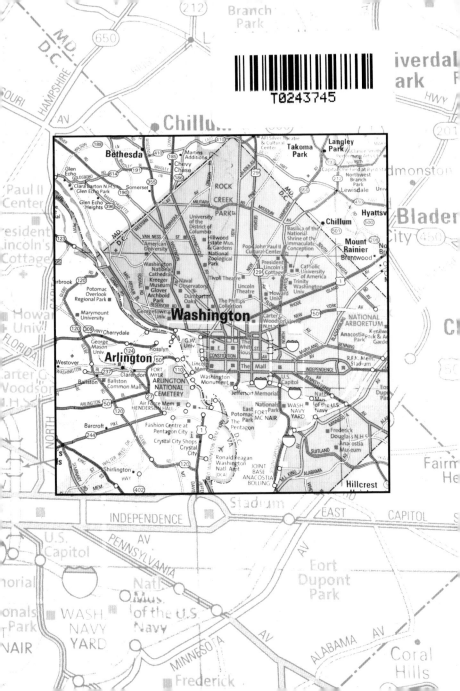

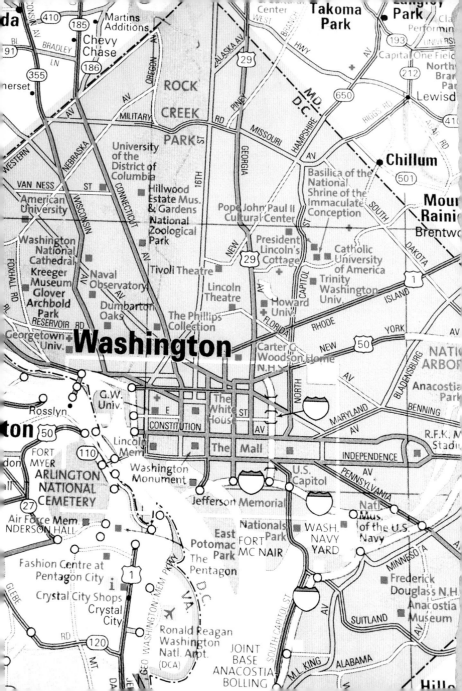

DC

COCKTAILS

AN ELEGANT COLLECTION OF OVER 100 RECIPES INSPIRED BY THE CAPITAL CITY

TRAVIS MITCHELL

CIDER MILL
PRESS

BOOK
PUBLISHERS

DC COCKTAILS

ISBN-13: 978-1-64643-443-5
ISBN-10: 1-64643-443-9

This book may be ordered by mail from the publisher. Please include $5.99 for postage and handling. Please support your local bookseller first!

Books published by Cider Mill Press Book Publishers are available at special discounts for bulk purchases in the United States by corporations, institutions, and other organizations. For more information, please contact the publisher.

Cider Mill Press Book Publishers
"Where good books are ready for press"
501 Nelson Place
Nashville, Tennessee 37214
cidermillpress.com

Typography: Bureau Eagle, Avenir, Copperplate, Sackers, Warnock

Photography credits on page 310

Printed in India

23 24 25 26 27 REP 5 4 3 2 1

First Edition

CONTENTS

INTRODUCTION

11th and F Street NW, early 20th century

When President George Washington founded the new federal district in 1790, he did so with land ceded from Maryland and Virginia. Much like the city itself, Washington's cocktail culture sits at a cultural crossroads of North and South.

During the summer months, locals take to patios in search of frozen drinks to cut the sweltering climate that would make a Floridian feel at home. Saturday and Sunday call for carefree brunches with bottomless bubbly drinks that would do New Orleans proud. And after dark, Washingtonians are as likely as New Yorkers to spend a night sipping Martinis and Manhattans in a dimly lit hotel lobby, or to admire the cocktail wizardry at a bartending hotspot.

Of course, as residents of the capital city, Washingtonians have a reputation for working as hard or harder than they imbibe. The cyclical nature of government and politics has also pegged D.C. with a reputation of being a city full of transplants and transients. A place where politicians, lawyers, and other leaders come to make their mark and then punch their ticket home once the job is done. There's some truth to that, but it's far from the entire story.

If anything, the ebb and flow of power brings a constant flow of new personalities and ideas. Access to embassies and other international institutions creates opportunities for festivals and specials. D.C. is constantly being gifted new experiences that provide the city's bartenders and cocktail industry a well of inspiration.

THE GIN RICKEY: A D.C. ORIGINAL

Of all the cocktails you'll find on D.C. menus, the humble Gin Rickey holds the most significance to locals. History suggests that the three-ingredient mix of gin, lime juice, and seltzer water was the invention of "Colonel Joe" Rickey during the summer of 1883. He would order up the refreshing highball at Shoomaker's Saloon, which was located at 1331 E Street NW and a haunt for politicos and other power brokers of the time. The drink was originally made with rye whiskey, before gin emerged as the go-to base spirit. Either way, it's a surefire weapon with which to battle back against the stale air of summer. The Rickey was recognized as the official cocktail of D.C. in 2011, and a yearly bartending competition pits the city's best against one another to come up with new takes on the simple formula.

Prohibition officers raiding a D.C. restaurant, 1923

ALONG COMES PROHIBITION

For the fourteen years from 1919 to 1933, the 18th Amendment banned the production and sale of alcohol across the United States. The District has a particularly deep tie to Prohibition. While most states went dry in 1920, D.C. got a head start on the nationwide detox with the passing of The Sheppard Bone-Dry Act in 1917. The bill was sponsored by Rep. Morris Sheppard, a Texas democrat whose name has inspired bars around D.C., both now and in the past.

In his book, *Prohibition In D.C.: How Dry We Weren't*, author Garrett Peck notes that not only did Washington get slapped with restrictions several years earlier than the rest of the country—it also rebelled against its expected duty as a role model for temperance to other states. Ironically, some of the very lawmakers who voted in favor of Prohibition were the biggest rulebreakers. Perhaps one of D.C.'s most infamous bootleggers was a man named George Cassiday. As official U.S. Senate history tells it, Cassiday, having returned from World War I,

View from the Capitol, west-southwest

began smuggling briefcases of liquor bottles to Capitol Hill at the request of friends. He was instantly recognized by his emerald hat, and his exploits went unquestioned by the Capitol Police for years. It was a slick system, but it wouldn't last forever.

Cassiday's trade started unraveling in 1929, when his years of illegal activity triggered a raid on his home. Officers seized 266 quarts of premium booze and none other than Vice President Charles Curtis himself ordered a sting operation that would put a stop to Cassiday's shenanigans. After placing Roger Butts, known as the "Dry Spy," within the Senate to monitor the activity, Prohibition agents caught Cassiday in a parking lot on February 18, 1930. "The Man with the Green Hat," as he had come to be known, was found with six bottles of gin along with a list with the names of his clientele—plenty of U.S. Senators included—and sentenced to eighteen months in prison.

Members of the legislative branch were far from the only ones looking to steal a swig of booze during the 1920s and 1930s. Speakeasies—illegal, unlicensed bars—began popping up across the city in response to prohibition, with thirsty Washingtonians meeting up for drinks wherever they could find them. In a 2014 article for *Smithsonian Magazine*, author Natasha Geiling writes that D.C.'s 267 licensed taverns ballooned into nearly 3,000 speakeasies. One prominent spot included the Mayflower Club on Connecticut Avenue, just south of Dupont Circle. Another rumored spot was Beuchert's Saloon on Capitol Hill, which reemerged in 2013 as a farm-to-table restaurant and cocktail bar. The one thing these locations had in common was the presence of strong, stiff liquor that was worth the effort it took to procure it.

After a more than seventeen-year dry spell, D.C. was freed from Prohibition restrictions. The 21st Amendment was adopted on December 5, 1933, and the date is still celebrated today. Each year, the D.C. Craft Bartenders Guild holds an opulent Repeal Day Ball full of drinking and 1920s-era inspired outfits.

Georgetown waterfront, early 20th century

Summertime baseball on the National Mall, 1942

Dupont Circle looking east

Logan Circle

Barrel (see page 220)

COCKTAILS IN CONTEMPORARY D.C.

D.C.'s many neighborhoods house a variety of cocktail bars, from historic power spots like Off The Record at the Hay Adams to industry hangouts like U Street's Service Bar. Legendary standbys exist, too, like Old Ebbitt Grill, the city's oldest running tavern, founded in 1856. Whether the vibe is fancy or fun, the quality of cocktails and bartenders across D.C. punches hard for a city of its size. There are fewer than 700,000 people living in D.C. proper, yet it has attracted some of the country's and the world's top talent.

In many ways, Washington's relatively small size is its greatest strength. For one, it fosters a bartending community that is tight-knit and supportive. There is friendship among competition, with trends and techniques shared often. It's common to see bars partnering up for special menus or collaborations, often highlighting out-of-town bartenders or a specific liquor or brand.

On the more practical side, the city's layout makes it easy to get from place to place and explore distinct neighborhoods without spending an hour in crosstown traffic. A home base in or around downtown, for example, is well positioned to hit drinking destinations like Adams Morgan, U Street, Shaw, and Penn Quarter on foot. Or start in Georgetown and soak up the charm and history of the city's oldest neighborhood while taking in views of the Potomac River. That's not to say anything about Capitol Hill, where the bars and restaurants along Pennsylvania Avenue and Barracks Row (the main stretch of 8th Street SE) have long been spots for after-work rounds among political staffers and interns. Not to be left out is the rapidly growing Union Market district, home to one of the best dives in town, Last Call, as well as the Cotton and Reed Distillery's award-winning rum.

Like other world cities, Washington's international influences have played a big role in shaping the bar scene here. There are bars that specialize in Japanese spirits, American and European whiskeys, agave spirits, and even things like Balkan rakia.

Of course, Washington's southern roots get plenty of nods on menus, too. Old Fashioneds are always in style, and warm-weather patio pounders like Aperol Spritzes and Mimosas flow freely during brunch hours and rooftop season. (A noticeable lack of skyscrapers makes rooftop drinking especially lovely in D.C., as it only takes a dozen or so floors to get sweeping views of downtown and the surrounding landscape.)

So whether your travels take you to a five-star hotel bar for a Sazerac, or a breathtaking rooftop to enjoy a spicy Margarita, or just a regular old corner bar for a well-made classic, you'll find that D.C. is a city that punches far above its class when it comes to bartending skill and quality.

ADAMS MORGAN

POWER MOJITO

JRDS WHISKEY SOUR

CITRUS CORDIAL LEMONADE

PINEAPPLE CARDAMOM
MILK PUNCH

OMAR'S FIZZ

STRAWBERRY SHORTCAKE

NOTORIOUS RBG

MULE D'OR

MIGS MACUÁ

Adams Morgan, the area along and around 18th Street NW, is one of the central arteries for D.C. cocktails and nightlife. The neighborhood name is derived from two formerly segregated elementary schools. Its colorful and quirky row houses provide character that matches that of the surrounding bars, from the Middle Eastern vibes of The Green Zone to the whiskey-lined back bar at Jack Rose Dining Saloon. Many businesses also have large patios ideal for warm-weather sipping and people-watching along the busy strip. After a round or two, you can wander over to one of the several pizza windows along the street, offering up D.C.-style jumbo slices that will satisfy late-night appetites.

An easy walk up from Adams Morgan via Columbia Road NW is Mt. Pleasant, a primarily residential neighborhood that's home to a few bars and restaurants notable for their craft. It's also accessible from the Columbia Heights metro station on the Green Line.

POWER MOJITO

ALFRESCO TAP AND GRILL
2009 18TH STREET NW

I f any cocktail could be considered "healthy," it's this Power Mojito from Adams Morgan newcomer Alfresco Tap and Grill. Managing Partner Cindy Sanchez says the drink honors the restaurant family's Cuban heritage while also incorporating a vitamin-packed, fiber-filled, and antioxidant-rich experience. It's a drink that will leave guests feeling as fresh as it tastes.

GLASSWARE: Collins glass

GARNISH: Slice of kiwi, mint sprig

- 1 oz. organic agave nectar
- 1 stem kale leaves, separated from the stalk
- 1 lime, peeled
- 5 to 6 mint leaves
- ¾ oz. dark rum
- Splash of seltzer water

1. Combine all of the ingredients, except for the rum and seltzer water, in a blender.

2. Place the blended mixture into a cocktail mixing tin.

3. Add rum and ice and shake until chilled and combined.

4. Transfer the mixture into a collins glass. Top it with seltzer water and garnish it with a kiwi slice and a mint sprig.

JRDS WHISKEY SOUR

JACK ROSE DINING SALOON
2007 18TH STREET NW

Jack Rose is the place to be for whiskey by the glass. Owner Bill Thomas has his bar stacked high with thousands of bottles from around the world, and price points range from affordable to splurge-worthy. There's also a small retail shop set up at the front of the restaurant where guests can purchase bottles to take home, including a rotating selection of exclusive picks. The cocktail program is equally impressive, with everything from syrups to juices and cordials made fresh. For a taste of Jack Rose at home, try this whiskey sour, made with egg white and a house special citrus cordial.

✧

GLASSWARE: Coupe glass

- 2 oz. bourbon
- 1 oz. egg white

- 2 oz. JRDS Citrus Cordial (see recipe)

1. Combine all of the ingredients in a cocktail shaker without ice.

2. Dry-shake for 10 to 20 seconds, then add ice and shake again, 10 to 20 seconds.

3. Pour into a coupe glass and serve.

JRDS CITRUS CORDIAL

- 1 lime peel
- 1 lemon peel
- ¾ cup lime juice
- ¾ cup lemon juice
- 1 teaspoon citric acid
- 1 ½ cups sugar
- 3 cups boiling water

1. Combine the peels, juices, acid, and sugar in a heatproof container.

2. Pour boiling water over all of the ingredients and mix well until the sugar has dissolved. The heat will pull the oil out of the peels.

3. Strain after everything has been mixed well.

0-ABV ALTERNATIVE: Citrus Cordial Lemonade

◇

GLASSWARE: Collins glass
GARNISH: Lime wheel

- 2 oz. JRDS Citrus Cordial
- 4 oz. sparkling water

1. Combine all of the ingredients in a collins glass.

2. Garnish with a lime wheel.

PINEAPPLE CARDAMOM MILK PUNCH

THE IMPERIAL
2001 18TH STREET NW

Michelin-honored The Imperial is the sister bar to Jack Rose, and it has a focus on cocktails that use creative and unique techniques. Known for creating an arsenal of interesting house ingredients, beverage director Joseph Oddo is showcasing this Pineapple Cardamom Milk Punch, which tricks the eye by delivering so many flavors in a crystal-clear cocktail.

GLASSWARE: Rocks glass

GARNISH: Lemon twist

- 10 pods of cardamom
- Peels of two lemons
- Peels of two oranges
- 29 oz. pisco
- 3 oz. crème de cacao

- 8 oz. lemon juice
- 8 oz. fresh pineapple juice
- 15 oz. simple syrup
- 8 oz. milk

1. Crack the cardamom pods to release their oils. Combine the pods, fruit peels, and pisco in a large mason jar.

2. Cook the mixture in sous vide at 135ºF for 2 hours. Strain the mixture and set aside. If you do not have a sous vide machine, you can let the infusion sit for about a week at room temperature, agitating it once a day.

3. Combine the cardamom-pisco mixture, crème de cacao, lemon and pineapple juice, and simple syrup in a large glass vessel.

4. Slowly add the milk and give it a good stir to incorporate. Allow the mixture to curdle then set it in the refrigerator overnight.

5. Set up a coffee filter to strain the mixture into your desired container for service. Strain the punch, 3 oz. at a time, into a mixing glass with ice, and stir until the punch is chilled and diluted.

6. Serve the punch in a rocks glass, over a big rock when possible, garnished with a lemon twist.

OMAR'S FIZZ

LAPIS
1847 COLUMBIA ROAD NW

The immigrant-owned Lapis translates traditional Afghan flavors into modern takes on food and drink. From the bar, guests can expect cocktails made with the country's signature ingredients. Omar's Fizz—a family name anagram of the Ramos Gin Fizz—is inspired by *firnee*, a custard dessert made with cardamom, pistachio, rosewater, and saffron. Created by bar manager Sulaiman Popal, Omar's Fizz carries deep and rich dessert notes that play well off the lightness coming from lemon and club soda.

GLASSWARE: Highball glass

GARNISH: Shiso leaves

- 1 ½ oz. saffron-infused Singani
- 1 oz. vanilla syrup
- 1 oz. lemon juice
- 1 oz. heavy cream
- 3 dashes cardamom bitters
- 1 egg white
- Splash of club soda, to top

1. Combine of the ingredients but the club soda in a cocktail tin and shake without ice.

2. Add ice and shake again until the mixture is chilled and combined.

3. Allow the drink to rest for 30 seconds, then strain it into a highball glass and top with club soda.

4. Garnish with shiso leaves.

STRAWBERRY SHORTCAKE

LAPIS

1847 COLUMBIA ROAD NW

As a kid, bar manager and second-generation Afghan immigrant to the U.S. Sulaiman Popal remembers being overwhelmed by the brownies, candy-filled cookies, pies, and other American desserts his aunts made. (They were determined to embrace their newly-adopted country through baking.) This cocktail is a tribute to his favorite aunt, who has long held the family title for the best strawberry shortcake.

GLASSWARE: Coupe glass

GARNISH: Flower

- 1 ½ oz. charred strawberry-infused pisco
- ¾ oz. vanilla syrup
- ¾ oz. lemon juice
- Graham Cracker Foam (see recipe), to top

1. Combine all of the ingredients, except for the foam, in a cocktail tin with ice and shake.

2. Serve the cocktail in a coupe.

3. Top it with graham cracker foam and garnish with a flower of choice.

GRAHAM CRACKER FOAM

Combine 5 oz. vanilla syrup, 4 oz. heavy cream, 4 oz. water, and 75 grams graham cracker crumbles in a bowl and allow the mixture to sit overnight. Strain and discard the solids. Add 2 egg whites to the batch and store it in a 16 oz. pressurized canister (cream whipper/dispenser). Shake the canister 25 times and chill for 1 hour before dispensing.

NOTORIOUS RBG

THE GREEN ZONE
2226 18TH STREET NW

The Green Zone has made its mark in D.C. by bringing interpretations of Middle Eastern cocktails and flavors to the nation's capital. Owner Chris Hassaan Francke uses ingredients like figs, pistachios, apricots, and pomegranate in his recipes, which play up classic cocktails from the Bee's Knees to the bar's signature Saz'iraq. The bar also has fun with tropical ingredients and boozy concoctions, like twists on the Hurricane and a frozen mint lemonade.

Named for the late Ruth Bader Ginsburg, this drink has flavors of funky Jamaican gold rum, banana, and ginger. It's a classic example of both the bar's politics and its love of rum and tropical flavors.

GLASSWARE: Cooler glass

GARNISH: 2 pineapple fronds

- 2 oz. Worthy Park Estate Rum-Bar Gold Jamaican Rum
- ¾ oz. pineapple juice
- ½ oz. Giffard Banane du Bresil
- ¾ oz. lemon juice
- ½ oz. honey-ginger syrup
- 1 dash absinthe
- 1 dash Angostura bitters

1. Using a device such as a milkshake machine, flash-blend all of the ingredients with crushed ice and two ice cubes.

2. Pour the mixture into a cooler glass and top with more crushed ice if necessary.

3. Add a straw and two pineapple fronds.

MULE D'OR

Co-owner Chas Jefferson says this cocktail embodies the spirit of Le Mont Royal: either take something trashy and make it fancy, or take something fancy and make it trashy. This recipe for a classic Mule, amplified by passion fruit liqueur, turns into summertime in a glass. The bar serves it on draft with fresh ginger, saffron-infused vodka, and forced carbonation. But even sticking with a standard vodka will produce a cocktail that is refreshing, tart, and spicy.

GLASSWARE: Highball glass

- 1 oz. Chinola Passion Fruit Liqueur
- 1 oz. vodka
- Juice of ½ fresh lime
- Ginger beer, to top

1. Combine the passion fruit liqueur, vodka, and lime juice in a highball with ice.

2. Stir to combine.

3. Top with a good-quality ginger beer.

MIGS MACUÁ

Lucky Buns' beverage director William Jackson named this variation on a Macuá—the official drink of Nicaragua—after his grandfather, a Nicaraguan immigrant. The tropical notes from the drink fit right in with Lucky Buns' feel-good vibes and the big, bold flavors coming out of chef Alex McCoy's kitchen.

GLASSWARE: Collins glass

GARNISH: Mint, cherry, cocktail umbrella

- 3 oz. pink guava nectar
- 1 oz. Flor de Caña 3-Year Rum
- ¾ oz. lemon juice
- ½ oz. London dry gin
- ½ oz. simple syrup
- ½ oz. Luxardo Maraschino Originale
- 2 dashes Bittermens Xocolatl Mole Bitters

1. In a cocktail shaker, combine all of the ingredients and shake with ice.

2. Strain the cocktail into a collins glass and top with crushed ice.

3. Garnish with mint, cherry, and a cocktail umbrella.

LOGAN CIRCLE/
14TH STREET

SNOW
EMERGENCY
ROUTE
NO PARKING DURING
EMERGENCY

SUN BREAKING THROUGH
THE FOG

SAVANNAH STAGE

GRAND DAME

PX OLD FASHIONED

FATHER JOHN

CLASSIFIED DOCUMENTS

ALMA DE MAIZ

EL NOPAL

This popular stretch of 14th Street starts south at Thomas Circle and stretches north to U Street. The namesake Logan Circle sits just to the east. It's where you'll find a pair of D.C.'s most influential bars—ChurchKey and The Gibson—which both emerged as hotspots in the mid-2010s when the craft cocktail and beer scene began to take hold throughout the city (and the world). While some of the storefronts have been occupied by national brands, there is still a lot to explore along this easy-to-stroll neighborhood. Take a manageable walk from the Dupont Circle (Red), McPherson Square (Blue), or U Street/African-American Civil War Memorial/Cardozo (Green) metro stations to explore.

SUN BREAKING THROUGH THE FOG

BRESCA
1906 14TH STREET NW

At Bresca, chef Ryan Ratino serves up elevated French-inspired food that's both modern and exciting. The bar program carries on that ethos, pulling techniques from across the history of cocktails. Bar director Will Patton uses Monet's famous impressionist painting as a muse for a rum drink with Tiki-esque vibes for this cocktail.

GLASSWARE: Collins glass

GARNISH: Yellow viola flower

- ¾ oz. Ten to One Caribbean Dark Rum
- ¾ oz. Fonseca 10-year Tawny Port
- ¾ oz. Amaro Montenegro
- ¾ oz. lime juice
- ¾ oz. Pineapple Syrup (see recipe)

1. Combine all of the ingredients in a cocktail shaker. Add ice and shake well, about 10 seconds.

2. Strain the cocktail over crushed ice.

3. Garnish with a yellow viola flower.

PINEAPPLE SYRUP

Combine equal parts pineapple juice and sugar in a blender and blend on high for 2 minutes. Let the syrup settle, then transfer it to a container for storage in the refrigerator until ready to use.

SAVANNAH STAGE

St. James brings modern Caribbean flare to D.C.'s vibrant U Street neighborhood. The Savannah Stage takes its name from the Caribbean Carnival in Trinidad and Tobago and invites the spirit of dressing up in costume and dancing through the island nation's annual celebration parades. For an authentic recreation, seek out some Trinidad-distilled Angostura 1919 Rum. Be sure to start making the Curry Mango Cordial a week ahead of time.

GLASSWARE: Rocks glass

GARNISH: 2 lime wheels

- 3 lime quarters
- 1 barspoon sugar
- 1 ¾ oz. Angostura 1919 Rum
- 1 oz. Curry Mango Cordial (see recipe)
- ¼ oz. Fee Brothers Fee Foam

1. Add the lime quarters and sugar to a cocktail shaker and lightly muddle.

2. Add the remaining ingredients and dry-shake for 10 seconds.

3. Add ice and shake for 15 seconds.

4. Double-strain the cocktail into a rocks glass over two lime wheels and ice.

CURRY MANGO CORDIAL

- 2 lbs. chopped mangos
- 175 grams white sugar
- 75 grams apricot preserves
- 500 ml 151 proof rum
- 300 ml fresh mango puree
- 1 tablespoon curry powder
- 100 ml water
- 1 habanero pepper, chopped
- 250 ml saffron liqueur

1. In a deep metal baking pan, combine the chopped mangos and sugar. Mix well.

2. Cover the pan with aluminum foil, then place it in a 320°F oven for 1 ½ hours. Remove the pan from the oven and let it cool.

3. Mix in the apricot preserves, then transfer the mixture to a large mason jar. Add the rum and allow it to infuse for one week. Strain and bottle the mango-rum mixture. Set aside for step 6.

4. In a medium saucepan, combine the mango puree, curry powder, water, and habanero. Stir then bring the mixture to a boil.

5. Reduce the heat to low and let simmer for 30 minutes. Remove the mixture from heat and let it stand overnight. In the morning, strain the curry-mango simple syrup through cheesecloth and bottle it. Set aside for step 6.

6. Combine 250 ml of the mango-rum mixture, 300 ml of the curry-mango simple syrup, and the saffron liqueur. Mix well. Strain the cordial and bottle it. Store it in the refrigerator unitl ready to use.

GRAND DAME

LE DIPLOMATE
1601 14TH STREET NW

A decade after opening its doors, Le Diplomate's plucked-from-Paris menu and decor continues to hold the awe and attention of D.C. diners, from neighborhood regulars to pop culture and political celebrities. The Grand Dame borrows from Europe and America, combining bourbon whiskey with the deep flavors of French and Italian vermouth.

GLASSWARE: Coupe glass

GARNISH: Orange peel

- 1 oz. Jim Beam Bourbon
- 1 oz. Tempus Fugit Gran Classico
- ½ oz. Guerin Rouge Dry Vermouth
- ½ oz. Punt e Mes

1. Combine all the spirits into a mixing glass and add enough ice so that the ice is slightly higher than the combined spirits.

2. Using your barspoon, stir everything vigorously for roughly 30 seconds.

3. Strain the contents of the mixing glass into a coupe.

4. Twist an orange peel over the cocktail, and use the skin side of the orange peel to rub around the entire rim. Then drop the orange peel into the cocktail.

PX OLD FASHIONED

CHURCHKEY/BIRCH & BARLEY
1337 14TH STREET NW

Taken together, ChurchKey's beer-focused bar and Birch & Barley's modern American dining room form a two-story power couple along 14th street. Cocktails are under the oversight of Neighborhood Restaurant Group spirits guru Nick Farrell. The PX Old Fashioned is the location's signature cocktail, a shift on something familiar made with local rye from KO Distilling in Manassas, Virginia. It's perfect to pair with some bar snacks or a hearty entrée—or simply to sip on when taking a break from the incredible library of draft and bottled beers.

GLASSWARE: Rocks glass

GARNISH: Orange peel, lemon peel

- 2 oz. KO Bare Knuckle Bottled-in-Bond Rye
- ½ oz. PX Simple Syrup (see recipe)

- 2 dashes Angostura bitters
- 1 dash orange bitters

1. Combine all of the ingredients into a cocktail tin with ice and stir until well chilled.

2. Strain the cocktail into a rocks glass over a large ice cube.

3. Garnish with an orange peel and a lemon peel.

PX SIMPLE SYRUP

Combine 200 ml hot water, 200 grams demerara sugar, 1 oz. PX Sherry, ¼ oz. Angostura bitters, ¼ oz. orange bitters, and a pinch of salt in a saucepan and bring the mixture to a boil. Stir until the sugar is dissolved then allow the syrup to cool completely before using.

IAN AND ERIC HILTON, THE GIBSON AND THE H2 COLLECTIVE

Brothers Ian and Eric Hilton have influenced seemingly all corners of the D.C. cocktail and bar scene. In 2009, they opened The Gibson, a speakeasy-inspired bar just off the busy intersection of 14th and U Street NW. Hidden behind an unmarked black door, The Gibson fostered the rebirth of craft cocktails in the city. The pair has also given Washingtonians hangouts for tacos and margaritas (El Rey), retro video games (Player's Club), and more.

In a sentence or two, how do you describe the cocktail culture of D.C.?

DC's cocktail culture is a real powerhouse these days. The incredible groundwork laid by bars like The Gibson, Room 11, Columbia Room, The Passenger, and so many others has fomented a knowledgeable customer base that is thirsty for more. Big names like Ryan Chetiyawardana (Silver Lyan) and Death & Co. are coming to town because our market has proven to be very desirable. Both tourists and locals alike have a plethora of amazing options for elevated drinking here now.

Your bars, especially The Gibson, have had an incredible impact on shaping the D.C. craft cocktail scene. What do you attribute that to? Was that the goal when you set out on this path?

The Gibson, as DC's first modern-era speakeasy, did a lot to elevate the drinking scene and bring it into the modern era. Our goal was to bring the cocktail renaissance into this market in a way that was true to both here as a hometown and to our aesthetic as owners. A bar that has great cocktails, a dark, sultry aesthetic, good music, and a place to sit down will never go out of style in our book. Fourteen years later, I would say we achieved our goals. The market here is fantastic, and The Gibson is still going as strong as ever!

What makes an outstanding bar program, in your opinion? What is the through line that connects your concepts together?

An outstanding bar program has to bring every element together, from the greeting at the front door to the cocktails themselves to the chair the customer is sitting in. If you have a phenomenal cocktail program but the hospitality is off and the ambiance isn't enjoyable, that's not going to be a winner. We try with all our concepts to let each bar be true to itself. We're not going to have customers waiting forever for complicated drinks in a packed club when they want to get back on the dance floor, and nobody wants to pay a premium price for an impeccably built, complicated cocktail only to have people jostling up against them while they try to enjoy it.

If you met someone who was new to D.C., what advice would you give them for exploring the city's bars and neighborhoods?

Get out of downtown and explore the city! There are fantastic gems that you will never find if you just stick to the tourist areas. Come up to U Street or 14th Street NW and wander around, find a bar you like the vibe of, and ask the bartender where else you should visit. Hospitality professionals are in the know, and they will be happy to share their wealth of knowledge with you.

FATHER JOHN

THE GIBSON
1705 14TH STREET NW

The Gibson helped to jumpstart D.C.'s modern cocktail era when it opened in 2009. The unmarked door, chalkboard specials menu, and warm lighting add up to a relaxed speakeasy vibe in one of the city's busiest nightlife neighborhoods. Former head bartender and general manager Frank Jones created and named this drink in honor of Father John Payne, a mentor and friend from his time as a student at the Duke Ellington School of the Arts.

GLASSWARE: Highball glass

- **1 oz. Plymouth Gin**
- **½ oz. Domaine de Canton (or other ginger liqueur)**
- **½ oz. cherry liqueur**
- **½ oz. Bénédictine**
- **1 egg white**
- **Ginger ale, to top**

1. Add all of the ingredients, except for the ginger ale, to a cocktail shaker.

2. Shake vigorously for 20 seconds without ice, then add ice and shake vigorously again.

3. Double-strain into chilled highball glass and slowly add ginger ale (it will foam).

CLASSIFIED DOCUMENTS

JANE JANE
1705 14TH STREET NW

Inspired by Southern hospitality and warm, inviting dinner parties among friends, Jane Jane bartenders are always eager to mix up a classic or reimagine something from the archives. With Classified Documents, Drew Porterfield uses celery juice to give the Gin Collins an herbal twist.

GLASSWARE: Highball glass

GARNISH: Lemon twist or cucumber ribbon

- 1 ½ oz. Rieger's Gin
- 1 ¼ oz. Clarified Celery Juice (see recipe)
- 1 oz. lemon juice
- ½ oz. simple syrup
- Sparkling water, to top

1. Add all of the ingredients to a cocktail shaker tin and shake for 30 to 45 seconds.

2. Strain the cocktail into a highball with fresh ice and top with a splash of sparkling water.

3. Garnish with a lemon twist or cucumber ribbon.

CLARIFIED CELERY JUICE

Juice one head of celery and weight the juice on a gram scale. Multiply the weight of the juice by .0025, then weigh out the same amount of Pectinex. Add the Pectinex to the celery juice and whisk vigorously for 1 to 2 minutes, or use an immersion blender and blend for 1 minute. Allow the mixture to rest in the refrigerator overnight. Strain the mixture through a coffee filter and store the clarified juice for up to 5 days before using.

ALMA DE MAÏZ

MAÏZ64
1324 14TH STREET NW

This spicy agave drink was the first cocktail that head bartender Roberto Andraca created for Maïz64. It was inspired by his memory of eating elotes con chili with his brothers on his father's farm in Guerrero, Mexico.

GLASSWARE: Coupe glass

- Tortilla Chili Salt (see recipe), for the rim
- 1 ½ oz. tequila or mezcal
- ½ oz. lemon juice
- ½ oz. lime juice
- 1 oz. Elote Chili Syrup (see recipe)

1. Combine all of the ingredients in a cocktail shaker with ice and shake.

2. Strain the cocktail into a coupe with fresh ice and a tortilla chili salt rim.

ELOTE CHILI SYRUP

Combine 250 grams sugar, 375 ml water, ¼ fresh corn cob, ¾ jalapeño pepper, and ½ morita pepper in a saucepan and bring the mixture to a simmer, simmering for 15 minutes. Blend the mixture, then strain it through a sieve. Allow the syrup to cool before storing it in the refrigerator.

TORTILLA CHILI SALT

Add 1 dry corn tortilla and 2 tablespoons salt to a blender and blend until combined.

EL NOPAL

Wanting a refreshing new addition to the cocktail menu, Andraca borrowed flavors from a salad that Maïz64 head chef Alam Méndez Florian prepared, which featured the bright, green notes of fennel and cactus. An agricole-style rum makes a good substitute for the Mexican rum.

GLASSWARE: Coupe glass

GARNISH: 2 spritzes of mezcal

- 1 oz. Mexican rum
- ¾ oz. Fennel-Cactus Syrup (see recipe)
- ¾ oz. lemon juice
- ½ oz. Ancho Reyes Verde Liqueur

1. Combine all of the ingredients in a shaker with ice and shake.

2. Strain the cocktail into a coupe and garnish with two spritzes of mezcal.

FENNEL-CACTUS SYRUP

Add 500 ml simple syrup, 60 grams clean, chopped cactus, and 50 grams fennel stems with leaves to a blender and blend until smooth.

COLUMBIA HEIGHTS/ MT. PLEASANT

ATLANTIC CITY

GIN GRIN

MADAME LEE

KIDS' CHOICE AWARDS

OAXACAN
BOTTLEROCKET

CHOCOLATE CITY
MANHATTAN

SPICY CALAMANSI
MARGARITA

Travel North from Logan Circle and you'll be in the heart of Columbia Heights, a dense neighborhood that is known for its Latin American businesses and hangouts. It's easily accessible by bus or metro, making it an ideal location in D.C. to string together a cocktail crawl. You'll find worthwhile blocks to explore as you continue north along 14th Street.

A short walk to the west is Mt. Pleasant, a primarily residential neighborhood that's home to a few bars and restaurants notable for their craft. It's an easy walk up from Adams Morgan via Columbia Road NW, and is also accessible from the Columbia Heights metro station on the Green Line.

ATLANTIC CITY

OKPB

3165 MT. PLEASANT STREET NW

David Strauss, creator of this cocktail along with Dylan Zehr, is a veteran of the D.C. cocktail scene, having cut ice and stirred drinks at the helm of some of the top speakeasy-inspired bars in the city. His current operation, OKPB, awaits visitors behind an unmarked door in the Mt. Pleasant neighborhood. The waitlist can get long during peak hours, but patience brings an escape to a world of precise mixology and a wealth of cocktail knowledge.

GLASSWARE: Rocks glass

GARNISH: Lemon peel

- 2 oz. apple brandy
- ½ oz. Luxardo Abano Amaro
- ½ oz. Lazzaroni Amaretto

1. Combine all of the ingredients in a rocks glass.

2. Add a large rock of ice and stir.

3. Express the oil from a long lemon peel and use the peel as a garnish.

GIN GRIN

OKPB
3165 MT. PLEASANT STREET NW

The Gin Grin makes its mark with tried-and-true flavors that are both light and lively. The easy drinking mix of Aperol, lemon juice, and mint is a simple and refreshing drink that's sure to brighten any occasion.

GLASSWARE: Rocks glass

GARNISH: Mint sprig

- ½ lemon
- 1 ½ oz. gin
- ½ oz. Aperol
- ¾ oz. simple syrup
- 2 dashes Angostura bitters
- 5 to 6 mint leaves

1. Muddle the lemon half in a cocktail shaker.

2. Add the remaining ingredients and shake short and vigorously.

3. Strain the contents of the shaker into a rocks glass and top with cracked ice.

4. Garnish with a mint sprig.

MADAME LEE

The menus at Queen's English are inspired by Hong Kong and the 156 years it spent as a British territory. The bar stocks a selection of baijiu, a clear Chinese spirit that's among the most consumed liquors in the world. In creating this spin on a Daiquiri, bar manager Tracy Eustaquio maintains the classic's clean and balanced profile while pumping up the flavor at every step. If you don't have purple carrots for the juice, regular orange ones will do.

GLASSWARE: Rocks glass

- 1 ½ oz. Pimm's No. 1
- ¾ oz. lime juice
- ¾ oz. simple syrup
- ½ oz. Jamaican rum
- ½ oz. purple carrot juice
- Barspoon rose water, to top

1. Add all of the ingredients, except for the rose water, to a shaking tin.

2. Fill the tin with ice and shake until chilled and diluted.

3. Strain the cocktail into a rocks glass with fresh ice. Float a barspoon of rose water on top.

KIDS' CHOICE AWARDS

Beverage director Chris Sang says he was inspired by a trip he took to a Chinese bakery in his New York hometown, where he tasted a mango pandan custard. This cocktail strikes up a balance between a shaken Piña Colada and cereal milk. Sang says guests appreciate the nostalgia—the bright green color recalls the green slime popularized by Nickelodeon's 1990s kids' shows.

GLASSWARE: Goblet or pint glass

- 1 ½ oz. Lockhouse Gin
- 1 oz. Mango Syrup (see recipe)
- ¾ oz. Pandan Coconut Milk (see recipe)
- ¾ oz. lemon juice

1. Combine all of the ingredients in a cocktail shaker over ice and shake well.

2. Strain the cocktail over pebbled ice into a goblet.

MANGO SYRUP

Cut fresh mangoes into cubes, then place them into a saucepan with equal parts water and sugar. Cook the mixture down until soft, then place it into a blender and blend until smooth. Strain the syrup.

PANDAN COCONUT MILK

Combine 150 grams sugar, 10 grams pandan leaf extract, and 1 can of coconut milk using an immersion blender.

OAXACAN BOTTLEROCKET

ROOSTER & OWL
2436 14ᵀᴴ STREET NW

The Oaxacan Bottlerocket is a tribute to Chris Sang's favorite cocktail, the Queen's Park Swizzle. Rather than using the traditional combination of spiced and overproof rums, Sang opted for similar components with a spice kick from a house-made syrup to pair with a base of mezcal and spiced rum. The spirit-forward drink is served over pebbled ice to soften the boozy punch.

GLASSWARE: Highball glass
GARNISH: Mint sprig

- **Handful of mint leaves**
- **¾ oz. Del Maguey Vida Mezcal**
- **¾ oz. Smith & Cross Jamaica Rum**
- **1 oz. lime juice**
- **¾ oz. Thai Chili Basil Syrup (see recipe)**
- **½ oz. falernum**
- **½ oz. orange juice**
- **Peychaud's bitters, to top**

1. Place the mint leaves at the bottom of a highball and fill with ice (ideally pebble ice).

2. Fill the glass with the remaining ingredients, except for the bitters, and top with more pebbled ice.

3. Top with Peychaud's bitters until you see a nice red layer on the top of the drink.

4. Garnish with a mint sprig.

74 — D.C. COCKTAILS

THAI CHILI BASIL SYRUP

Make 16 oz. of simple syrup by combining water and sugar over heat in a 1:1 ratio. Let the simple syrup cool completely, then infuse it with 10 grams of Thai chile pepper and one-quarter of a pack of Thai basil.

CHOCOLATE CITY MANHATTAN

PURPLE PATCH
3155 MT. PLEASANT STREET NW

A classic Manhattan is the perfect canvas for showcasing the D.C. region's local spirits. In this take, Purple Patch opts for rye whiskey from Virginia's Catoctin Creek Distilling Company, accenting it with Italian amaro, sweet vermouth, and two types of bitters: black walnut and Aztec chocolate.

GLASSWARE: Coupe glass

GARNISH: Luxardo cherry

- 2 oz. Catoctin Creek Roundstone Rye
- ½ oz. sweet vermouth
- ¼ oz. Braulio Amaro
- 1 dash Fee Brothers Black Walnut bitters
- 1 dash Fee Brothers Aztec Chocolate bitters

1. Combine all of the ingredients in a mixing glass with ice.

2. Stir 25 rotations, until the drink is chilled and combined.

3. Strain the cocktail into a coupe and garnish with a Luxardo cherry.

SPICY CALAMANSI MARGARITA

PURPLE PATCH
3155 MT. PLEASANT STREET NW

This house cocktail, a Purple Patch favorite, has been on the menu since 2015. It spotlights calamansi, a Filipino citrus fruit that tastes like a mashup of lemon, lime, and mandarin orange. You can find calamansi extract or calamansi honey at the Purple Patch market or at Filipino markets. The "spicy" comes courtesy of jalapeno-infused tequila.

GLASSWARE: Old-fashioned glass
GARNISH: Lime wedge

- 1 ½ oz. Jalapeño-Infused Tequila (see recipe)
- ½ oz. triple sec
- ½ oz. lime juice
- 1 ½ oz. calamansi sour mix

1. Combine all of the ingredients in a cocktail shaker with ice and shake.

2. Strain the cocktail into an old-fashioned glass with fresh ice and garnish with a lime wedge.

JALAPEÑO-INFUSED TEQUILA
Roast jalapeño peppers (as many as desired), then place them in one bottle of tequila blanco and let them infuse the tequila for 3 to 5 days.

SHAW

APRICOT MEETS CORN

HARVEST TIME

GOTTA ROLL

THE DABNEY MARTINI

SAMUELSSON

AJI DAIQUIRI

Michelin-starred restaurants, cozy wine bars, and lively outdoor patios are just some of what you'll discover in the diverse streets and alleys of the Shaw cocktail scene. Shaw has long been the place to find the city's edgier bars and restaurants, like the pisco-focused bar Amazonia or the longtime favorite Whitlow's, which relocated from its longtime Northern Virginia home in 2022. Shaw is served by the metro Green Line and is close to the U Street and Chinatown/Penn Quarter neighborhoods.

APRICOT MEETS CORN

AMBAR SHAW
1547 7TH STREET NW

A Balkans-inspired Manhattan, this drink introduces guests to the world of rakia, a type of fruit liquor popular across Balkan countries. It also makes use of apricot and corn, two ingredients found in the region. Ambar Shaw uses Dolin Rouge but any sweet vermouth will work; apricot brandy can be substituted for the rakia.

GLASSWARE: Rocks glass

GARNISH: Orange peel, cherry (optional)

- 1 oz. apricot rakia
- 1 oz. bourbon
- ½ oz. Dolin Rouge Vermouth
- ½ oz. Nixta Licor de Elote
- 3 dashes orange bitters

1. Combine all of the ingredients in a mixing glass. Add ice and stir for at least 30 seconds.

2. Strain the cocktail into a rocks glass, over a large cube ice.

3. Express the orange peel over the drink and garnish with the orange peel and a cherry (if using).

HARVEST TIME

AMBAR SHAW
1547 7TH STREET NW

Whiskey, lemon, and honey are a tried-and-true base for the Harvest Time, which celebrates quince rakia, an essential rakia variety. The cocktail is meant to be both playful and refreshing. Quince brandy can be substituted for the rakia if needed.

GLASSWARE: Rocks glass

GARNISH: Mint leaves, shaved nutmeg

- 1 oz. Monkey Shoulder Scotch Whisky
- 1 oz. quince rakia
- ¼ oz. Honey Syrup (see recipe)
- ¾ oz. Ginger Syrup (see recipe)
- ¾ oz. lemon juice

1. In a cocktail shaker with ice, combine the whiskey, rakia, the syrups, and the lemon juice. Shake well for at least 30 seconds.

2. Strain the cocktail into a rocks glass over fresh ice.

3. Garnish with a mint leaf, gently smashing the leaf to release its aromas, and grate fresh nutmeg over the top.

HONEY SYRUP

Combine equal parts honey and water in a saucepan and bring the mixture to a gentle boil, stirring until the honey is dissolved. Remove the syrup from heat and allow it to cool.

GINGER SYRUP

Peel a handful of chopped ginger root and cut it into small pieces. Transfer the ginger to a saucepan, cover it with water, and bring it to a boil. Boil until the ginger pieces soften, 10 to 15 minutes. Place the ginger in a blender, then add ½ cup simple syrup and a pinch of turmeric. Blend everything very well and strain the mixture through a sieve, using a spatula to push ginger fibers into the sieve so that all of the juices are extracted from the fibers. Let the syrup cool before transferring it to a storage container.

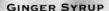

GOTTA ROLL

BOUNDARY STONE
116 RHODE ISLAND AVENUE NW

Boundary Stone brings a welcoming, warm pub feel to D.C.'s Bloomingdale neighborhood, just a bit north and west of Shaw. The story behind the Gotta Roll, the longest-running cocktail on the bar's menu, centers around long-time friend of the bar R.B. Wolfensberger. Along with his wife, Meghan Brown, Wolfensberger is also the owner and founder of Gray Wolf Craft Distilling in Saint Michaels, Maryland, which makes the gin used in this shaken drink. The name of the gin and cocktail were further inspired by the Phish song "Timber (Jerry the Mule)." Kayla Langston crafted this recipe.

GLASSWARE: Coupe glass

GARNISH: Lemon peel

- 1 ½ oz. Timber Sassafras Rested Gin
- ¾ oz. fresh-squeezed lemon juice
- ½ oz. elderflower liqueur
- ¼ oz. Triple Syrup (see recipe)

1. Combine all of the ingredients in a cocktail tin and shake well until chilled and combined.

2. Double-strain the cocktail into a coupe.

3. Garnish with a lemon peel (dehydrated, if you prefer).

TRIPLE SYRUP

Combine four parts simple syrup (1:1), two parts agave, and one part honey and mix well.

THE DABNEY MARTINI

THE DABNEY
122 BLAGDEN ALLEY NW

Chef Jeremiah Langhorne's refined mid-Atlantic menu and open-hearth cooking make his restaurant one of D.C.'s most sought-after dining reservations. With a Michelin star to its name, you can be sure The Dabney's cocktail program is just as thoughtful as the plates coming out of the kitchen. Bar Manager Dan Todd's version of the classic Martini is brightened up with homemade tincture of satsuma mandarins, sourced from Bhumi Growers in New Jersey.

GLASSWARE: Martini glass, chilled
GARNISH: Maple hibiscus leaf

- 2 oz. Ki No Bi Kyoto Dry Gin
- ½ oz. Mancino Secco Vermouth
- ½ oz. Mancino Bianco Vermouth
- 1 dash Satsuma Mandarin Tincture (see recipe)
- Expressed lemon peel

1. Combine all of the ingredients, except for the lemon peel, in a mixing glass and fill the glass with ice.

2. Stir for 20 to 25 seconds and strain into a well-chilled martini glass or coupe.

3. Express and discard a lemon peel over the cocktail and drop in a maple hibiscus leaf to garnish.

SATSUMA MANDARIN TINCTURE

Thinly slice mandarins into wheels and dehydrate them. In a glass jar, combine 20 grams of the dehydrated mandarins with 100 grams neutral grain spirits and let the mixture sit out for at least 60 days. Fine-strain the tincture into a glass dasher bottle.

SAMUELSSON

MAXWELL PARK
1336 9TH STREET NW

Wine is the primary draw at this cozy bar, thanks to a regularly changing menu offering themed finds in pours sized from 2 ½ oz. to a bottle. If the urge for something a little stronger strikes, bartenders here are glad to mix up a classic cocktail or a house favorite. One of their specialty drinks is the Samuelson, an oily, herbal, and savory Rum Sour that creator and Maxwell Park owner Brent Kroll says was inspired by flavors he had while dining at one of chef Marcus Samuelsson's restaurants.

GLASSWARE: **Rocks glass**

- **2 oz. Peanut-and-Dill-Infused Smith & Cross Rum**
- **½ oz. lemon juice**
- **½ oz. demerara simple syrup**

1. Combine all of the ingredients in a shaker with ice and stir well until chilled.

2. Strain the cocktail into a rocks glass over fresh ice.

PEANUT-AND-DILL-INFUSED SMITH & CROSS RUM
Infuse 1 (750 ml) bottle of Smith & Cross Jamaica Rum by adding peanuts for 3 days. Steep with fresh dill for a few hours to finish, then strain before using or storing.

AJI DAIQUIRI

THE ROYAL
501 FLORIDA AVENUE NW

A cafe by day and cocktail hang by evening, The Royal has garnered attention from the Michelin guide for its takes on Latin American food and drinks. The Aji Daiquiri has been a mainstay on the cocktail menu. The key here is the addition of Colombian aji sauce, which gives green, herbaceous notes to the already fresh and clean rum Daiquiri formula. Chimichurri can be substituted for the aji sauce.

GLASSWARE: Coupe glass, chilled

GARNISH: Cilantro sprig

- 2 oz. white rum
- 1 oz. fresh lime juice
- ½ oz. simple syrup
- ¼ oz. Aji Sauce (see recipe)

1. Combine all of the ingredients into a cocktail shaker with ice and shake well, about 30 seconds.

2. Strain into a chilled coupe and garnish with a small sprig of cilantro.

AJI SAUCE

Combine 5 seeded jalapeño peppers, ¾ cup chopped green onions, ½ cup chopped cilantro, 2 tablespoons water, 2 tablespoons white vinegar, 2 tablespoons fresh lemon juice, and 1 teaspoon salt in a blender. Blend until combined, then strain the sauce into a container or use immediately.

U STREET

CAPTAIN CODY

STARRY NIGHTS

WATCH YOUR SPEED

FLOWER CHILD

Once known as "Black Broadway," U Street is historically rich with live music venues and theaters, family-owned restaurants, and plentiful spots for a cocktail. Many Washingtonians come to this neighborhood to catch a show at the 9:30 Club or to cap a night out with a half-smoke and fries from Ben's Chili Bowl. Its proximity to Howard University and the Green Line metro also makes it a popular destination for students. The U Street bar scene offers lively nightlife and dancing, and peaks on weekends, when sidewalks are filled with revelers.

CAPTAIN CODY

ARCHIPELAGO
1201 U STREET NW

The Captain Cody is this U Street oasis's take on the Painkiller formula of rum, pineapple, and cream of coconut. Owner Owen Thompson worked to balance the sweetness of orange juice by using both pineapple juice and pineapple shrub—the latter giving a nice acidity to the final product.

GLASSWARE: Tiki mug

GARNISH: Anything tropical and fun, freshly grated nutmeg

- 1 oz. Appleton Estate Jamaican rum
- 1 oz. Wray & Nephew Overproof Rum
- ¾ oz. Pineapple Shrub (see recipe)
- ¾ oz. Coco López Cream of Coconut
- ¾ oz. pineapple juice
- ½ oz. orange juice

1. Combine all of the ingredients in a cocktail mixing tin with 4 to 6 oz. crushed ice.

2. Give the mixture a quick shake. (Archipelago spins their version with a milkshake stick mixer.)

3. Dump the contents into your tiki mug of choice and fill with more crushed ice.

4. Garnish with something festive, such as an orange slice, pineapple slice, fronds, or an umbrella, and then grate fresh nutmeg over the top.

PINEAPPLE SHRUB

Combine equal amounts of shredded pineapple, white wine vinegar, water, and sugar in a saucepan and bring the mixture to a boil. Stir to dissolve the sugar. Remove the shrub from heat and let it cool before straining it into a container and storing it in the refrigerator.

STARRY NIGHTS

Chad Spangler, Glendon Hartley, and Christine Kim have created an oasis of cocktails in one of D.C.'s essential nightlife districts. It's a high-volume bar that shakes and pours drinks to crowds all night while still feeling low-key and personal. The staff here are knowledgeable about classics and always pushing new flavors and combinations. And true to its name, Service Bar has carved out a niche as a hangout for D.C. bar professionals who come for its happy hours and industry-focused events.

This drink was born while Spangler was bartending at Chaplin's, before Service Bar opened. He had enjoyed the taste of Wray & Nephew White Overproof Rum and its many pronounced flavors, such as coconut, nutmeg, and anise. Bourbon brings additional spice and vanilla notes to the party for a tropical, spirit-forward feel. Stick to the brand names here, as deviating from them won't result in the same cocktail. Fresh mint is a must, too. Spangler also gives a tip for adding the bitters—hold the bottle horizontally rather than turning it upside down for better control of the amount in the glass.

GLASSWARE: Rocks glass

GARNISH: Mint sprig

- 1 ½ oz. Wild Turkey 81 Proof Bourbon
- ½ oz. Wray & Nephew White Overproof Rum
- ¼ oz. demerara syrup
- 2 short dashes Angostura bitters
- 4 to 5 fresh mint leaves

1. Add all of the ingredients to a mixing glass. Lightly tap, but don't muddle, the mint leaves.

2. Add ice to above the level of the liquid and stir for about 30 seconds.

3. Once the liquid is thoroughly chilled, strain the cocktail into a rocks glass over a large ice cube.

4. Garnish with a mint sprig.

WATCH YOUR SPEED

Whitlow's history spans decades, with its original location having opened in downtown D.C. in 1946. After closing in 1989 to make way for a development project that never materialized, the business reopened in 1995 in Arlington as Whitlow's on Wilson, where it became a popular neighborhood gathering spot. The bar changed spaces again in 2022, when it brought its hospitality to the lively Shaw neighborhood. This cocktail, Watch Your Speed, is inspired by the Espresso Martini and uses both a local Virginia coffee and a Maryland-distilled coffee liqueur.

GLASSWARE: Coupe glass, chilled

- 2 oz. vanilla vodka
- 1 oz. McClintock Distilling Co. Coffee Liqueur
- 1 ½ oz. Coffee Syrup (see recipe)
- 2 dashes Woodford Reserve Bourbon Barrel Aged Chocolate Bitters

1. Combine all of the ingredients in a cocktail shaker.

2. Shake vigorously, then strain the cocktail into a chilled coupe glass.

COFFEE SYRUP

Brew a concentrated batch of coffee using two bags of Swing's Coffee G Street Blend. Put the brewed coffee in a saucepan and add demerara sugar at a ratio of 1 cup sugar for every 1 cup coffee. Bring this mixture to a gentle boil, stirring constantly to dissolve the sugar, then lower the heat and let simmer for 3 minutes. Let the mixture cool, then pour the syrup into a glass jar. It will keep for up to 3 weeks.

FLOWER CHILD

LUCY BAR
1350 FLORIDA AVENUE NW

Bartender—and creator of this recipe—Bratislav Glisic has quite a resume, including an influential role at the award-winning team at Employees Only in New York. His work at Lucy Bar brings this passion for mixology to the Mediterranean menu of house-made pizzas, pastas, and small plates.

GLASSWARE: Nick & Nora glass

GARNISH: Star anise

- 1 ½ oz. Hine VSOP Cognac
- 1 oz. lemon juice
- 7/10 oz. hibiscus syrup
- ½ oz. Bénédictine
- ½ oz. aquafaba

1. Pour all of the ingredients into a mixing glass, add ice, and shake.

2. Strain the cocktail into a Nick & Nora glass.

3. Garnish with star anise.

CAPITOL HILL

THE DIEGO RIVERA

A STONE'S THROW

THE BELTWAY BOY

THE SWAMPOODLE

THE WELLS MARTINI

THE ENZONI

On Capitol Hill, wide avenues and historic government buildings (the Capitol dome being the prime example) give way to sweeping views filled with quaint row houses and quiet streets. Government workers and Hill staffers frequent the bars along Pennsylvania Avenue and 8th Street SE, many of which specialize in serving well-made classics in cozy taverns and historic settings that are quintessentially D.C. Capitol Hill is the place to sip on an Old Fashioned or a nice pour of bourbon while catching a view into the city's political side.

THE DIEGO RIVERA

BEUCHERT'S SALOON
623 PENNSYLVANIA AVENUE SE

This neighborhood restaurant and cocktail bar is a revival of a tavern that originally opened in 1880 and was rumored to have operated a speakeasy during Prohibition. These days, though, there's nothing secret about the menu of farm-to-table cooking and thoughtfully crafted classic cocktails. The Diego Rivera is beverage director Mackenzie Conway's mezcal-forward take on a Hemingway Daiquiri.

GLASSWARE: Coupe glass

- 2 oz. Banhez Espadin Mezcal
- ¾ oz. Luxardo Maraschino Originale
- 1 oz. grapefruit juice
- ½ oz. lime juice

1. Combine all of the ingredients in a cocktail shaker.

2. Shake vigorously until chilled and combined.

3. Double-strain into a coupe.

A STONE'S THROW

Beverage director Mackenzie Conway says this tossed cocktail has off-dry flavors similar to a Manhattan, with a rich texture from the Barolo Chinato, a piney anise note from the mastiha, and a boozy rye spice thread that cuts through both. It was named in honor of Nick Benson and Paul Russo, two legendary stone carvers and Beuchert Saloon regulars who run the John Stevens Shop and do all the hand-carved letters for the Smithsonian.

GLASSWARE: Coupe glass

GARNISH: Lemon twist

- 1 ½ oz. Sazerac 6 Year Old Rye Whiskey
- ¾ oz. Barolo Chinato
- ¾ oz. Skinos Mastiha Spirit

1. Combine all of the ingredients in a medium cocktail shaker.

2. Next to it, prepare a large cocktail shaker filled with ice.

3. Using a julep strainer on top of the large tin, pour the contents of the medium tin over the ice. Next, toss the liquid through the julep strainer back into the small tin.

4. Repeat this tossing process three or four times until enough dilution occurs to fill a 5 oz. coupe.

THE BELTWAY BOY

BEUCHERT'S SALOON
623 PENNSYLVANIA AVENUE SE

This drink is a staple at Beuchert's Saloon, combining the best of the Sazerac and the Boulevardier. It was first stirred up by Brendan McMahon for the bar's opening menu back in 2013.

GLASSWARE: Coupe glass

GARNISH: Expressed orange peel

- Absinthe, for the rinse
- 1 oz. Foro Amaro
- 1 oz. Aperol
- 1 oz. Old Overholt Rye Whiskey
- 5 dashes Peychaud's bitters

1. Combine all of the ingredients together in a mixing glass with ice.

2. Stir well, about 30 seconds.

3. Strain into an absinthe-rinsed coupe.

4. Garnished with an orange expression.

THE SWAMPOODLE

No matter the city, Irish pubs are ideal gathering spots for low-key drinks. The Dubliner is no exception. Established in 1974, it's been pouring pints and mixing cocktails for nearly 50 years. You can go classic or branch out with a featured option like The Swampoodle, a drink named for an old Irish neighborhood not far from the Capitol building. Beverage director and creator of this cocktail Donato Alvarez says the combination of tea, honey, Cardamaro, and sweet vermouth creates a luxurious, bittersweet backdrop for the Irish whiskey's mellow and refined profile.

GLASSWARE: Nick & Nora glass

- 1 ¼ oz. Dubliner Irish Whiskey
- ¾ oz. Cardamaro Vino Amaro
- ½ oz. Dolin Sweet Vermouth
- ½ oz. lemon juice
- ½ oz. Irish Breakfast Honey Syrup (see recipe)

1. Combine all of the ingredients in a shaker.

2. Shake well until the mixture is combined and chilled.

3. Double-strain the cocktail into a Nick & Nora, coupe, or martini glass.

IRISH BREAKFAST HONEY SYRUP

In a small saucepan, bring 6 oz. water to simmer. Add two bags of Irish tea and steep for 2 minutes, then discard them. Stir in 6 oz. honey until it has dissolved. Once the syrup has cooled, transfer it to a glass jar and refrigerate before use.

THE WELLS MARTINI

THE WELLS
727 C STREET SE

At The Wells, gin is always in. This intimate cocktail bar, within walking distance of D.C.'s Eastern Market, stocks gin bottles from around the world, encompassing many different styles and flavor profiles. Don't be shy about asking for more information about something that looks unfamiliar. Danya Degen's savory take on a Martini uses a clever olive oil–infused gin along with some saline for a briny, dirty taste— no olives necessary.

GLASSWARE: Martini glass

GARNISH: Expressed orange peel, 4 drops olive oil

- **2 oz. Olive Oil–Washed Gin (see recipe)**
- **1 oz. Cocchi Americano**
- **5 drops Saline Solution (see recipe)**

1. Build all of the ingredients in a cocktail shaker with ice and stir until well chilled.

2. Pour the cocktail into a martini glass or coupe.

3. Garnish with an expressed orange peel and four drops of olive oil.

SALINE SOLUTION

Combine a 1:1 ratio of kosher salt and hot water, stirring until the salt is completely dissolved.

Combine 4 oz. olive oil with a 1-liter bottle of gin and blend to emulsify. The mixture shoul look milky. Chill the mixture in the refrigerator for 2 hours. Strain the washed gin through a fine-mesh strainer and store it in the refrigerator until ready to use.

THE ENZONI

The Negroni is one of the more popular classic cocktails these days, and that's especially true at a gin-forward bar such as The Wells. Looking to explore lesser-known options, the bar introduced a take on the Enzoni, a somewhat obscure cocktail that uses grapes, gin, and red bitter liqueur, among other ingredients. It fits in nicely, as pastry chef Rochelle Cooper is especially fond of Concord grapes. This version uses grape shrub instead of pulp, and the acidity is balanced with a splash of vanilla syrup and a touch of shaved nutmeg. The bar suggests using a grape-based gin, such as Nordés, for fullest effect.

GLASSWARE: Rocks glass

GARNISH: Shaved nutmeg

- **2 oz. Grape Shrub (see recipe)**
- **1 ½ oz. gin**
- **¾ oz. Campari**
- **½ oz. lime juice**
- **½ oz. vanilla syrup**

1. Combine all of the ingredients in a cocktail shaker and shake vigorously until well chilled.

2. Strain the cocktail twice through a strainer.

3. Pour over ice into a rocks glass and garnish with shaved nutmeg.

Grape Shrub

If the grape pulp you're using is frozen, thaw it out overnight. Add 680 grams concord grape pulp, 400 grams white sugar, and 475 ml champagne vinegar to a container, cover it, and store it at room temperature for 5 days. Blend the ingredients with a hand mixer or immersion blender. Add an equal amount of water, then add the shrub to a blender and blend until combined. Strain the shrub through a fine-mesh strainer, transfer it to a storage container, and keep it refrigerated until ready to use.

BEAT OF THE DRUM

SPICED MAPLE MANHATTAN

4 GRAPES

FRENCH ART FILM

ABSINTHE RICKEY

CLASSIC PEAR MARTINI

A SENATOR'S SECRET

MINT JULEP

Unlike other major world cities, Washington's downtown is hard to define. The freeing absence of towering skyscrapers affords D.C.'s many office buildings and apartments to spread across a large footprint rather than a single business center. Much of the bar and restaurant action is clustered around K Street NW, known for being the address of choice for lobbyists, law firms, and think tanks. But that doesn't mean the streets are all work and no play. The steady stream of business activity supports a crop of fantastic cocktail bars, many of which are located inside chic hotels that are themselves worth exploring.

BEAT OF THE DRUM

ALLEGORY
1201 K STREET NW

Its location in the Eaton hotel library gives Allegory the literary thread that runs through its cocktails. At the center of the experience is a concept menu, Down the Rabbit Hole, that invites guests to experience drinks from some of D.C.'s most talented bartenders through the lens of author Lewis Carroll's novel *Through the Looking-Glass*. There's a deeper element to the overarching theme, too, involving civil rights activist Ruby Bridges, who was the first black student to desegregate William Frantz Elementary School in Louisiana in 1960. With Beat of the Drum, bar director Deke Dunne embodies the moment of both these stories when the main characters, Alice and Ruby, begin to forge their own paths in life. Substitute any blanco or reposado tequilas as needed.

GLASSWARE: Coupe glass

GARNISH: Sprinkle of amaranth

- ¾ oz. Olmeca Altos Plata Tequila
- ¾ oz. Olmeca Altos Reposado Tequila
- ¼ oz. ruby port
- ¼ oz. oloroso sherry
- ¾ oz. fresh lime juice
- 1 oz. Mesoamerican Orgeat (see recipe)
- Barspoon fresh huckleberries

1. Combine all of the ingredients in a shaker tin, add ice, and shake vigorously for 10 seconds.

2. Double-strain the cocktail through a fine mesh strainer into a coupe.

3. Garnish with sprinkled amaranth and enjoy.

Mesoamerican Orgeat

Add 15 grams puffed amaranth, 50 grams quinoa, 5 grams cinnamon sticks, and 3 grams ground mace to a pan and slightly toast on very low heat until they emanate a rich baked smell. Blend the mixture, then add it to water and let it soak for 24 to 48 hours. Strain the mixture through a cheesecloth. Add 400 grams water and 800 grams sugar to a saucepan over medium heat. Incorporate the spice mixture, stirring until the sugar is fully dissolved. Let the syrup sit out to cool. Place it in a container and store in the refrigerator for up to 2 months.

SPICED MAPLE MANHATTAN

CENTRAL MICHEL RICHARD
1001 PENNSYLVANIA AVENUE NW

Amid what seems like a constant ebb and flow of businesses, Central Michel Richard's modern and fun French cooking remains a constant in downtown D.C. Much like the food, this Spiced Maple Manhattan injects tradition with enough of a fresh touch to keep things interesting.

GLASSWARE: Coupe glass, chilled

GARNISH: Brandied cherries

- 1 ¾ oz. Elijah Craig Rye Whiskey
- ¾ oz. Rabarbaro Zucca Amaro
- ½ oz. Spiced Maple Simple Syrup (see recipe)
- 3 drops orange bitters

1. Combine all of the ingredients in a cocktail shaker.

2. Add ice and stir 30 to 45 seconds, until chilled.

3. Strain the cocktail into a chilled coupe, straight up.

4. Garnish with brandied cherries.

SPICED MAPLE SIMPLE SYRUP
Combine 1 cup maple syrup, 1 cup spring water, 2 cinnamon sticks, and 1 clove in a saucepan and bring the mixture to a soft boil over medium heat. Simmer on low for 30 minutes. Chill the syrup in an ice bath. Strain the syrup through cheesecloth and refrigerate until ready to use.

4 GRAPES

In this elegant and effervescent cocktail, Versus Hospitality beverage director Hank Bowers finds a way to feature grapes in four different ways: pisco liquor, verjus, a cava-based syrup, and a delightfully playful cotton candy grape foam to top it all off. It's just the right amount of sophistication and whimsy for its rooftop location overlooking downtown D.C.

GLASSWARE: Nick & Nora glass
GARNISH: Cotton Candy Grape Foam (see recipe)

- 1 ½ oz. Caravedo Pisco
- 1 oz. verjus
- 1 oz. Cava Syrup (see recipe)

1. Combine all of the ingredients in a cocktail shaker and shake until combined.

2. Double-strain the cocktail into a Nick & Nora.

3. Garnish with the foam.

CAVA SYRUP

In a large pot or saucepan, combine 1 quart cava and 1 quart white sugar and bring the mixture to a boil. Let it simmer until the volume has reduced by half and the smell of alcohol is gone. Let the syrup cool then use or store it in the refrigerator.

FRENCH ART FILM

For a typical service, bar staff at Ciel Social Club spend nearly eight hours preparing this fizzy and fruity cocktail, made with passion fruit liqueur and vanilla-infused vodka. The mixture is left to sit overnight so that the milk can clarify before it's strained and kegged for quick service—a key strategy for the high-volume bar program. At home, though, the process can be shortened to a couple of hours.

GLASSWARE: Highball glass

GARNISH: Ice sphere, dehydrated passion fruit

- 1 ½ oz. Vanilla-Infused Vodka (see recipe)
- 1 oz. passion fruit puree
- 1 oz. Vanilla Syrup (see recipe)
- 9/10 oz. milk
- ½ oz. Chinola Passion Fruit Liqueur
- ½ oz. lime juice
- Champagne or sparkling wine, to top

1. Combine all of the ingredients, except for the Champagne, in a cocktail shaker or mixing glass and stir.

2. Wait 2 hours and then strain the mixture through a cheesecloth.

3. Pour the cocktail into a highball and top with Champagne.

VANILLA-INFUSED VODKA

Slice two vanilla beans and place them in 1 ¾ liters vodka. Then place the mixture in a plastic bag to sous vide at 155°F for 2 hours. Let the mixture cool and strain it into a container.

VANILLA SYRUP

Using a ratio of one vanilla bean to one quart of simple syrup, heat the mixture to a boil, remove it from heat, then let it steep for 15 minutes. Let the syrup cool then strain it into a container for storage.

ABSINTHE RICKEY

The joyous energy of New Orleans runs through all corners of Dauphine's. The restaurant is known for its homemade charcuterie, butchery, and seafood along with a menu of cocktails reminiscent of a night out in the Big Easy. After sipping on a Hurricane or a Sazerac, consider the bar's interpretation of the Rickey, which remains true to the dry and tart original while introducing absinthe and high-quality creme de menthe for a bold and fresh taste. This is a concoction by Donato Alvarez, beverage director, and Neal Bodenheimer, partner and beverage program creator.

GLASSWARE: **Highball glass**

GARNISH: **Grated cinnamon**

- ½ lime
- 2 oz. Kübler Swiss Absinthe
- ½ oz. Tempus Fugit Crème de Menthe
- 1 oz. Fever-Tree Club Soda

1. Squeeze the lime juice into a highball and drop the lime shell in the glass.
2. Add the absinthe, crème de menthe, and club soda to the glass.
3. Fill the glass with pebble ice and swizzle gently for approximately 5 seconds.
4. Pack more pebble ice on top and garnish with grated cinnamon.

CLASSIC PEAR MARTINI

OFF THE RECORD
800 16TH STREET NW

ocated inside the luxury Hay-Adams hotel, Off the Record is a favorite haunt among the city's political power players. The hushed
space is heavy with old-school Washington vibes, and its proximity to
the White House means you never know who you might see perched
at the bar for a classic Old Fashioned or Martini. This drink is the
most popular cocktail at Off the Record, by far. Bartenders say that on
a busy night, at least every table and bar spot orders at least one. The
bartender who originally created this cocktail has since moved on, but
the essence of the drink remains the same—with an updated interpretation thanks to food and beverage director Alex Roig. Roig, who
enjoys creating his own home infusions and syrups, took an interest in
the inclusion of pineapple in the drink's original build. Feeling that the
tropical fruit overpowered the pear, he opted to use an artisanal pear
nectar and remove the pineapple from the drink entirely.

GLASSWARE: Martini glass

GARNISH: Pear slice

- **2 oz. Grey Goose La Poire Vodka**
- **1 oz. St-Germain Elderflower Liqueur**
- **2 oz. William's Pear Nectar**
- **¼ oz. lime juice**
- **¼ oz. Chambord**

1. In a cocktail shaker filled half-way with ice, combine the vodka, St-Germain, pear nectar, and lime juice.

2. Shake the mix and strain it into a martini glass.

3. On the edge of the glass, pour the Chambord, and garnish with a slice of pear.

A SENATOR'S SECRET

OFF THE RECORD
800 16TH STREET NW

When he's home from the bar, Roig enjoys a classic Old Fashioned while nibbling on popcorn. But while his personal tastes have led him to adore the flavors of the bourbon world, he definitely has a sweet tooth. He and his team thus created A Senator's Secret, a sweeter take on a bourbon sipper. Old Forester is preferred here because it was the first bourbon to be bottled in 1870 and one of a handful of companies given a permit to bottle and sell during Prohibition.

GLASSWARE: Rocks glass

GARNISH: Cinnamon stick

- 2 oz. Old Forester Bourbon
- ½ oz. pear brandy
- ¼ oz. cinnamon syrup
- 3 dashes orange bitters
- Caramel Popcorn (see recipe)

1. In a mixing glass filled three-fourths of the way with ice, combine the bourbon, pear brandy, cinnamon syrup, and orange bitters.

2. Strain into a rocks glass over a 2-inch ice cube.

3. Garnish with a cinnamon stick and drink while nibbling the prepared Caramel Popcorn.

CARAMEL POPCORN

- ½ cup clear corn syrup
- 2 cups brown sugar
- 1 teaspoon salt
- ½ teaspoon baking soda
- 1 cup (2 sticks) unsalted butter
- 1 teaspoon vanilla extract
- 8 cups popped popcorn

1. Preheat the oven to 200°F. Prepare a rimmed baking sheet sprayed with oil.

2. In a large skillet or saucepan over medium heat, melt the butter.

3. Once the butter melts, add the corn syrup, brown sugar, and salt, stirring frequently until everything is dissolved and blended.

4. Keep stirring until the mixture starts to boil, around 10 minutes or so.

5. Once it starts to boil, set a timer for 2 minutes exactly and stir until your timer goes off.

6. After the timer goes off, remove the mixture from heat immediately and stir in the baking soda and vanilla.

7. At this point, your mixture will turn a light caramel color and expand. Keep stirring until the color is uniform and the texture is smooth, for a few more minutes.

8. Pour the sticky, thick caramel all over your popcorn in your large bowl.

9. Use a spoon or spatula to turn the popcorn gently while still moving quickly, until all of your popcorn is fully coated.

10. Once each kernel is coated in caramel, pour it from your large bowl onto your prepared baking sheet and spread out the popcorn as much as possible.

11. Bake in the oven for 45 minutes, allowing the caramel to set and harden evenly. Stir your popcorn every 12 minutes, breaking up clumps as best you can, until done.

MINT JULEP

Nicknamed the "Great Compromiser" for his legislative efforts to bring together the North and the South, Kentucky statesman Henry Clay is believed to have first introduced the Mint Julep to Washingtonians at the Willard Hotel, known at the time as the City Hotel, in the 1830s. That legacy lives on today at the hotel's Round Robin Bar, where this classic refresher awaits in old school Washington surroundings.

GLASSWARE: Tall glass

GARNISH: Mint sprig, lemon twist, sugar

- 4 to 6 mint leaves
- 1 teaspoon sugar
- 1 oz. sparkling water
- 2 oz. Maker's Mark

1. Add four to six mint leaves, the sugar, part of the sparkling water, and a small measure of bourbon to a tall glass.

2. Muddle gently.

3. Add crushed ice and mix gently.

4. Add more crushed ice and top off the cocktail with the remaining bourbon and water; mix gently.

5. Garnish with a mint sprig, lemon twist, and a dusting of sugar.

DUPONT CIRCLE

UNCLE IN BEL-AIR

YUKI'S GIBSON

LEFT OF SPRING

PRELUDE TO A KISS

THE PEPPERBOX

SAGWA MARTINI

THE BELMONT

GLITTA FADES

Forming the intersection between Massachusetts, Connecticut, and New Hampshire Avenues, Dupont Circle takes on characteristics of both urban and residential living. Its energy radiates out from its central park and fountain, where residents gather for chess matches, impromptu yoga sessions, or simply to pause over lunch and a good book. Each June, Dupont Circle becomes the place to be for the city's annual Pride Parade and festivities. Bars in this part of town are well-versed in classics, often drawing up seasonal variations to appeal to regulars and tourists.

UNCLE IN BEL-AIR

THE JEFFERSON HOTEL
1200 16TH STREET NW

This winter sipper from the bar at the uber-luxury Jefferson Hotel is served over ice, but it's packed with warming flavors. Bartender Chrissy Sheffey creates an icy take on hot cider with a body of whiskey, apple butter syrup, allspice dram, citrus, and Drambuie. Feel free to substitute a stemless wine glass for the rocks glass.

GLASSWARE: Rocks glass

GARNISH: Dehydrated apple slice, grated cinnamon

- 1 ½ oz. Uncle Nearest 1884
- ½ oz. allspice dram
- ½ oz. Drambuie
- ¾ oz. Apple Harvest Tea–Infused Apple Butter
- ¼ oz. lemon juice

1. Combine all of the ingredients in a cocktail shaker over ice and shake until chilled and combined.

2. Strain the cocktail into a rocks glass over fresh ice.

3. Garnish with a dehydrated apple slice and grated cinnamon.

YUKI'S GIBSON

DOYLE

1500 NEW HAMPSHIRE AVENUE NW

This gin-based cocktail balances sweet and floral notes from plum sake with the spice and warmth of pink peppercorn vermouth. An edible flower garnish ties the package together for an elegant and sophisticated sip.

◇

GLASSWARE: Coupe glass, chilled

GARNISH: Edible flowers

- 1 ½ oz. Japanese gin
- 1 oz. plum sake

- 1 oz. Pink Peppercorn–Infused Dry Vermouth (see recipe)

1. In a mixing glass, add all of the ingredients.

2. Fill the mixing glass with ice and stir until well chilled.

3. Strain the cocktail into a chilled coupe glass.

4. Garnish with edible flowers.

PINK PEPPERCORN–INFUSED DRY VERMOUTH

Crush ¼ cup pink peppercorns lightly with a mortar and pestle or rolling pin. Add the crushed peppercorns to 1 (750 ml) bottle dry vermouth and seal the bottle. Shake the bottle well to distribute the peppercorns evenly and let it sit at room temperature for 24 to 48 hours, depending on how strong you want the infusion to be. Strain the infused vermouth through a cheesecloth or fine-mesh strainer into a glass bottle or jar. Store in the refrigerator until ready to use.

LEFT OF SPRING

IRON GATE
1734 N STREET NW

This light Last Word riff calls forward Mediterranean vibes that gel with Iron Gate's Greek and southern Italian atmosphere. It uses mastiha, a refreshing, minty and vegetal Greek spirit made from the sap of an evergreen tree. The bar also highlights local gin from Republic Restoratives.

GLASSWARE: **Coupe glass, chilled**

- **1 oz. Dissent Gin**
- **¾ oz. mastiha**
- **¾ oz. génépy**
- **¾ oz. lime juice**

1. Combine all of the ingredients in a cocktail shaker filled with ice.

2. Shake hard until the mixture is chilled and combined.

3. Strain the cocktail into a chilled coupe.

PRELUDE TO A KISS

Paying homage to the 1938 classic ballad composed by Duke Ellington, Taha Ismail, director of food and beverage at the Ellington Park Bistro in the St. Gregory Hotel, wanted to showcase his creative take on a beloved classic sour cocktail. The infused gin with butterfly pea blossom and black tea leaves serves as the backbone, while the botanical flavor of lavender and crème de violette balanced with egg whites enhances this cocktail to be well balanced on the palate.

GLASSWARE: Coupe glass

- 1 ½ oz. Empress 1908 Gin
- ¾ oz. fresh lime juice
- ½ oz. Dolin Dry Vermouth de Chambery
- ¼ oz. Chambord
- ½ oz. Giffard Crème de Violette
- ½ oz. Lavender Syrup (see recipe)
- ½ oz. egg white

1. Combine all of the ingredients in a shaker without ice. Dry-shake the ingredients to combine.

2. Add ice to the shaker and shake again until well chilled.

3. Double-strain the cocktail into a coupe.

Combine 250 grams sugar, 250 grams water, and 1.25 grams dried lavender in a saucepan over medium heat and bring the mixture to a boil, stirring until the sugar has dissolved. Let cool before storing or using it.

THE PEPPERBOX

MCCLELLAN'S RETREAT
2031 FLORIDA AVENUE NW

Sitting at the north end of Dupont Circle, McClellan's Retreat takes its name from the Union Civil War general whose statue is perched nearby. The bar is outfitted with a serious selection of whiskeys from around the world ready to be enjoyed in cocktails or 1 ½ oz. tasting pours. One of the bar's signature drinks is the Pepperbox. Named after the multi-barrel nineteenth-century firearm, the cocktail is a mezcal-smoky twist on a Revolver.

GLASSWARE: Rocks glass
GARNISH: Habanero Ice Cube (see recipe)

- 1 ½ oz. Del Maguey Vida Mezcal
- ½ oz. cacao nib syrup
- ¼ oz. Lucano Caffè Liqueur
- 3 dashes Regans' Orange Bitters

1. Combine all of the ingredients in a shaker and stir well until chilled.

2. Pour into a rocks glass over a Habanero Ice Cube.

HABANERO ICE CUBE
Steep one sliced habanero pepper in 4 cups hot water for 30 seconds. Strain the water into ice molds, adding one habanero ring to each well, and freeze.

158 — D.C. COCKTAILS

SAGWA MARTINI

ANJU

1805 18TH STREET NW

Anju is among D.C.'s most sought-after reservations, with diners clamoring for its spicy, funky, and comforting Korean dishes. Behind the bar, Phil Anova mixes up drinks to pair with the kitchen's bold favors. His Sagwa Martini, served batched at the restaurant, uses a base of Calvados and Bénédictine against notes of lemon, lime, and apple puree.

GLASSWARE: Martini glass

- 2 oz. Daron Calvados
- 1 oz. Bénédictine
- ½ oz. simple syrup
- ¼ teaspoon ground gochugaru
- ¼ oz. lemon juice
- ¼ oz. lime juice
- 1 tablespoon apple puree
- ½ oz. absinthe, for the glass rinse

1. Combine all of the ingredients, except for the absinthe, into a shaker with ice and shake.

2. For the absinthe wash, add the absinthe to an empty martini glass and swirl a few times to coat. Pour out the remaining alcohol.

3. Strain the shaker mixture into the absinthe-washed martini glass through a fine mesh strainer.

THE BELMONT

This cocktail is a riff on the Boulevardier, a three-ingredient classic and the whiskey-based cousin to the Negroni. The drink's name comes from the Civil War battle fought in November 1861. The recipe includes rich herbal notes that play off the spice notes of the rye whiskey.

GLASSWARE: Rocks glass

GARNISH: Orange peel

- ¾ oz. WhistlePig PiggyBack 100% Rye
- ¾ oz. Boomsma Cloosterbitter
- ¾ oz. Angostura amaro
- ¼ dropper of Crude "Big Bear" Coffee & Cocoa Bitters

1. Combine all of the ingredients in a rocks glass over a large ice cube.

2. Stir well until the cocktail is chilled.

GLITTA FADES

The bar at Lyle's offers familiar cocktails prepared with gentle twists. The Glitta Fades was originally created to celebrate D.C. Pride, which energizes the city each June. The drink is vibrant and tangy, fitting for the lively atmosphere the annual festival brings to nearby Dupont Circle.

GLASSWARE: Coupe glass, chilled
GARNISH: Rainbow candy flag

- 2 oz. Republic Restoratives Civic Vodka
- ¾ oz. blueberry lavender syrup
- ½ oz. crème de violette
- ¾ oz. lemon juice
- ½ oz. egg whites

1. Combine all of the ingredients in a shaker and shake.
2. Double-strain the cocktail into a chilled coupe.
3. Garnish with a rainbow candy flag.

UNION MARKET/ IVY CITY

PISCO MORADA

MADEIRA FLIP

SA OLD FASHIONED

VALKYRIE

COCONUT DAIQUIRI

THE MAYAHUEL

WHERE THERE'S SMOKE

APEROL SCHLITZ

Union Market has come on strong in recent years thanks to development of new apartments and revitalized commercial and industrial real estate. The namesake food hall is the primary draw, though it's no longer the only reason to make a trip to the Northeast D.C. neighborhood. There's also La Cosecha, a Latin American–inspired market with everything from casual tacos and empanadas to Michelin-starred dining rooms, and spots to sip local spirits and beer. A short drive away is Ivy City, anchored by the reimagined Hecht Warehouse and also home to several worthwhile breweries and distilleries.

PISCO MORADA

Like the rest of the Serenata menu, the Pisco Morada celebrates the heritage and ingredients of Latin America. This adult take on Peru's purple-corn-based chicha morada beverage introduces pisco, medium-dry sherry, and a lemon-rosemary simple syrup. The violet-hued sipper grabs the attention of shoppers, diners, and other passersby at La Cosecha marketplace. Andra "AJ" Johnson crafted this cocktail.

GLASSWARE: Martini glass

GARNISH: Angostura bitters, dehydrated lemon wheel

- 1 ½ oz. Quebranta Pisco
- ¾ oz. lemon-rosemary-infused simple syrup
- ½ oz. Las Endrinas Pacharan/Chicha Morada Blend
- ¼ oz. medium-dry sherry
- ¼ oz. lemon juice
- 1 egg white

1. Dry-shake all of the ingredients together in a shaker tin.

2. Open the shaker tin and add ice.

3. Shake vigorously.

4. Strain the cocktail into a martini glass.

5. Once the foam settles, garnish with Angostura bitters and a dehydrated lemon wheel.

MADEIRA FLIP

ST. ANSELM
1250 5TH STREET NE

Built in the image of the classic American tavern, St. Anselm excels in wood-grilled meats, seafood, and comfort sides like its fluffy, indulgent biscuits. The bar program includes a lengthy list of drinks and spirits, including a selection of sherry and madeira—two types of fortified wines that were especially popular in the early days of the U.S. This simple Madeira Flip is an approachable way to mix up an old-school cocktail ingredient. Substitute any semi-sweet Madeira for the St. Anselm.

GLASSWARE: Nick & Nora glass

GARNISH: Freshly grated nutmeg

- 1 ½ oz. St. Anselm Single Barrel Madeira
- 1 whole egg
- ½ oz. demerara syrup

1. Add all of the ingredients to a cocktail shaker.

2. Shake with ice and strain the cocktail into a Nick & Nora.

3. Garnish with freshly grated nutmeg.

SA OLD FASHIONED

ST. ANSELM
1250 5TH STREET NE

St. Anselm's house version of this quintessential tavern drink uses a split base of bourbon and rum, two of the most important spirits throughout American history. Jamaican and spiced rum bring funk and complexity to the sweetness of the bourbon, and the use of allspice dram imparts the warming notes of baking spice.

GLASSWARE: Rocks glass

GARNISH: Lime wheel, orange twist

- 1 oz. Elijah Craig Bourbon
- 1 oz. Maggie's Farm Spiced Rum
- ¼ oz. Smith & Cross Jamaica Rum
- ¼ oz. Cotton & Reed Allspice Dram Rum
- ¼ oz. demerara syrup
- 3 dashes Angostura bitters

1. Combine all of the ingredients in a cocktail tin with ice.

2. Stir the mixture over ice until combined and chilled.

3. Strain the cocktail into a rocks glass and garnish with a lime wheel and an orange twist.

VALKYRIE

DISTRICT MADE SPIRITS
1135 OKIE STREET NE

Founders Sandy Wood and Alex Laufer built District Made Spirits to be a true grain-to-glass distillery. Their rye-based spirits showcase local farmers, and that commitment to agriculture and terroir creates drinks with truly distinctive character. This smoky and spicy complex cocktail was created by Andra "AJ" Johnson, who has worked at some of D.C.'s top bars, including Serenata at La Cosecha, where she is beverage director and managing partner. The Valkyrie pairs amaro and fig's dark and moody flavors with a hint of citrus and the spice-box notes of District Made Rye.

GLASSWARE: Rocks glass
GARNISH: Orange peel

- 1 ½ oz. District Made Rye Whiskey
- ¾ oz. of Amaro Montenegro
- 1 dash Angostura bitters
- ¾ oz. Apricot-Fig Simple Syrup (see recipe)
- 1 dash orange bitters

1. Use a blowtorch or long-handled lighter to set fire to your preferred smoking wood (apple wood is a good choice in this case).

2. Set a rocks glass upside down over the smoking wood chips to capture the smoke while you make the cocktail.

3. Combine all of the ingredients in a cocktail shaker or mixing glass filled with ice.

4. Stir until chilled and combined.

5. Strain the cocktail into the smoked rocks glass over a large ice cube.

6. Garnish with an orange peel.

APRICOT-FIG SIMPLE SYRUP

In a medium saucepan, add 8 oz. water and 8 oz. sugar. Heat at a low temperature, stirring intermittently to incorporate the sugar. When the mixture is transparent, add ¼ cup dried apricots and ¼ cup mission figs. Raise the temperature to medium, until it starts to boil. Lower the temperature and let the syrup simmer for 10 to 12 minutes. When the figs and apricots start to float, turn off the heat. Strain the syrup into a nonreactive container and let it cool before use.

COCONUT DAIQUIRI

COTTON & REED DISTILLERY
1330 5TH STREET NE

Although it originated in Cuba, the Daiquiri made its debut in the States at the Army & Navy Club in D.C.'s Farragut Square—a tie-in that fits when making the simple drink with this local spirit. This variation uses the distillery's Coconut Rum, which is made using about one-third lb. of dried organic coconut flakes per bottle. That natural coconut flavor, along with a touch of oil viscosity, brings balance to the drink's tart lime backbone.

GLASSWARE: Coupe glass, chilled

GARNISH: Lime wheel

- 2 oz. Cotton & Reed Coconut Rum
- 1 oz. fresh lime juice
- ¾ oz. simple syrup

1. Combine all of the ingredients in a cocktail shaker.

2. Add ice and shake until chilled and diluted.

3. Strain the cocktail into a chilled coupe.

4. Garnish with a lime wheel (dehydrated, if you prefer).

JAMES SIMPSON, DESTINO

1280 4TH STREET. NE

James Simpson grew up in the D.C. area and has spent twelve years working in the city's bar industry after a decade in Charleston, South Carolina, as part of what he saw as a larger trend of bartenders making the migration from south to north. He currently oversees bar operations at Destino, an agave-heavy program at La Cosecha, a Latin-focused market and food hall in Northeast D.C.

How do you describe the cocktail culture of D.C.? What are its strengths and signatures?

D.C. has been exploding and really strengthening its repertoire for culinary experiences and cocktail bars. Different ethnicities are coming into the city and opening up restaurants. So you have a classic city, one that is all about the cliches—the steakhouse, the Martini, the Rickey—to where we are in the present day. We have places like Daru, which is a great cocktail bar at the end of 15th and H, doing this modern Indian take on everything. Where I am at La Cosecha in Union Market we have Destino, this Latin bar that really is pretty agave heavy. We're right next to Serenata, which does a Caribbean rum feel. And then Mezcalero in the corner is just getting started. It feels like we are reinventing the classic D.C.

What would you say is your signature as a bartender? What is the through line or philosophy that shapes your menus and concepts?

What I try to do here is translate the ingredient or the spirit or the liqueur in the best way possible. I've got a Tepeztate mezcal where the plants took forty to forty-five years to grow. That's every day, somebody cultivating and walking up this mountain and tending to this plant. And then after forty years they harvest this plant and drag it down the hill. They go through an extremely labor-intensive process to produce this mezcal, which is just hundreds and hundreds of hours of work. To get it all the way to my bar is just an insane amount of craftsmanship, effort, and hard sweat equity that people have invested. And I could just ruin it by trying to make it too fancy or by just getting in the way of that product.

That also leads to our buying philosophy. We have to know who makes it; they have to be reinvesting in their community from both a sustainability perspective and also paying their workers well and, with agave spirits, it has to be owned by Mexicans. We always say, "We keep the money in the bottle."

Another undercurrent of D.C. cocktail bars is that the clientele here, the people that live here, are really interested in education. They're really interested in learning what's behind each one of these bottles. At the end of the day, we see people sitting down at our bar now that are calling for spirits that are really obscure.

What advice would you give to home bartenders looking to up their game?

The one thing I bring when I go to people's houses, especially if it's people who aren't necessarily in the industry and I know I'm going to probably have to make the cocktails, is ice. Everybody has sugar at the house. Everybody's limes and lemons are pretty standard. But bad ice from an old ice maker just destroys the drinks. I always recommend people buy the 1 x 1 cubes or bigger 2 x 2 cubes just to have at home. You can make yourself a nice Negroni or Old Fashioned very quickly with a big ice cube and it just really dresses it up.

THE MAYAHUEL

DESTINO
1280 4TH STREET NE

Destino takes its name from the many culinary journeys that shaped the restaurant's ethos and menu. Mexican spices and ingredients form a through-line, and drinks here are heavy on agave spirits, each thoughtfully sourced from Mexican-owned producers. Feel free to substitute a margarita glass for the coupe.

GLASSWARE: Coupe glass, chilled

- 1 ½ oz. El Buho Espadin Mezcal
- ¾ oz. Combier Liqueur d'Orange
- ¾ oz. fresh-squeezed lime juice
- ¼ oz. "Nogave" Syrup (see recipe)
- Chili salt, for the rim

1. Add all of the ingredients to a cocktail shaker filled with ice and shake vigorously.
2. Strain the cocktail into a chilled coupe with chili salt on the rim.

"NOGAVE" SYRUP

Place four parts cane sugar and one part honey into a saucepan or small pot. Add water at a 1:1 ratio to the sugar and honey mixture. Stir to combine over low heat and let the syrup cool before using.

WHERE THERE'S SMOKE

GRAVITAS
1401 OKIE STREET NE

Having earned its first Michelin star in 2019, Gravitas has become a D.C. destination for elegant American cooking, service, and cocktails. Chef Matt Baker heads up the kitchen and the drinks are under the wing of Judy Elahi. A girl scout in her youth, Elahi created the Where There's Smoke to remind people of camping. Not only is the drink smoked, it's also topped with a whiskey-soaked marshmallow made by the pastry team.

GLASSWARE: Rocks glass, wood-smoked
GARNISH: Whiskey-soaked marshmallow

- 1 ½ oz. Bar Hill Tom Cat Gin
- ½ oz. Bertola Sweet Vermouth
- 3 drops Bénédictine
- 2 dashes Angostura bitters
- 1 dash Peychaud's bitters

1. Combine all of the ingredients in a cocktail shaker over ice.

2. Stir 30 to 45 seconds until combined, chilled, and diluted.

3. Strain the cocktail over a large rock into a wood-smoked rocks glass.

4. Spray a peated whiskey over a marshmallow and use the marshmallow as a garnish.

GINA CHERSEVANI, LAST CALL

Gina Chersevani is known around D.C. for drinks that are balanced, creative, and unpretentious. Her concepts in the city's Union Market neighborhood include the no-frills Last Call, with Old Fashioneds on tap and spiked Jell-O molds in the fridge, and Suburbia, an airstream trailer specializing in refreshing frozen drinks.

How do you describe the cocktail culture of D.C.? What are its biggest strengths?

The culture in D.C. is young, which makes it fun—people are willing to try more. I love Washington, D.C., because it's an ever- changing canvas.

What makes an outstanding bar program, in your opinion?

It's simple: know your strengths and play to them.

What would you say is your signature as a bartender? What is the through line or philosophy that shapes your menus and concepts?

My signature style is "light and floral." I love pretty drinks that dance on your palate. My philosophy is more of a question. I always ask myself, "Would I order this cocktail for a second time?" If you would get another of the same, it's a keeper. If not, then you have work to do.

If you met someone who was new to D.C., what advice would you give them for exploring the city's bars and neighborhoods?

If you are new to Washington, D.C., take it neighborhood by neighborhood. There are so many great places scattered across the city that you can discover a vast array of cocktail destinations in almost every area.

APEROL SCHLITZ

LAST CALL BAR
1301-A 4TH STREET NE

At Last Call, Gina Chersevani has created a space that's as welcoming to a cocktail party as it is to a couple of beers and a round of shots. Her Union Market bar is rustic, clamoring with neighborhood regulars and all-in-all a no-worries hangout that won't blow a budget. Chersevani crafted this recipe.

⟡

GLASSWARE: Pint glass

GARNISH: Orange slice

- 1 ½ oz. Aperol
- 5 oz. Schlitz Beer

1. Pour Aperol into cocktail tin, fill the tin with ice, and shake.

2. Strain the Aperol into a pint glass filled with fresh ice.

3. Top with Schlitz beer and give it a half stir.

4. Garnish with an orange slice.

H STREET NE

IMMUNE BOOSTER

FAIRY TALE

CAPRI FIZZ

MATCHA DO ABOUT
NOTHING

CHERRY WHISKEY SOUR

The landscape of H Street's Northeast neighborhood is defined by historic brick rowhouses set alongside newer construction. These modern touches include the D.C. streetcar, which connects the stretch with Union Station to the west and Benning Road to the east. The majority of bars in this part of town are small businesses, and that feeling comes across in the creativity and affordability of options. It's also a relatively less-traveled bar scene and a nice contrast to tourist-filled parts of the city.

IMMUNE BOOSTER

STABLE
1324 H STREET NE

Alpine decor and hearty Swiss fare set the scene at Stable, and its gooey, cheesy fondue is among the city's best comfort food escapes when the temperatures turn frigid. The bar menu makes use of fruity, herbal liqueurs that are common in Switzerland. A standard of the restaurant's medicinal-inspired cocktails is the Immune Booster, which packs high levels of vitamin C and antioxidants. This recipe comes from Silvan Kraemer.

GLASSWARE: Rocks glass

GARNISH: Lemon peel

- 2 oz. Old Forester 86 Bourbon
- 1 oz. Rosehip Syrup (see recipe)
- ½ oz. lemon juice
- ¼ oz. raspberry schnapps

1. In a cocktail shaker with ice, combine all of the ingredients and shake well.

2. Strain the cocktail over one large ice cube into a rocks glass.

3. Garnish with a lemon peel.

ROSEHIP SYRUP

Combine 250 ml water, 200 grams white sugar, and 3 organic rosehip tea bags in a saucepan. Bring the mixture to a boil and stir until the sugar is dissolved. Remove the syrup from heat and let it infuse for 12 hours. Strain the syrup into a jar or other vessel.

FAIRY TALE

STABLE
1324 H STREET NE

Keeping on the theme of highlighting Swiss products, the Fairy Tale uses absinthe as its base. It's meant to be refreshing and absinthe-forward, allowing the spirit's character and unique flavor profile to shine through. For anyone visiting in person, Stable offers a full selection of absinthe cocktails and pours to explore. This recipe comes from Silvan Kraemer. Substitute any dry and floral white wine for the sauvignon blanc.

GLASSWARE: Coupe glass, chilled

GARNISH: Lemon peel

- 1 oz. Kübler Absinthe
- ½ oz. Republic Restoratives Civic Vodka
- ½ oz. sauvignon blanc
- 1 oz. lemon juice
- 1 oz. Lemon Simple Syrup (see recipe)
- 1 dash Angostura bitters

1. Combine all of the ingredients in a cocktail tin with ice.
2. Shake for about 10 seconds.
3. Double-strain the cocktail into a chilled coupe.
4. Garnish with a lemon peel.

LEMON SIMPLE SYRUP

In a saucepan, combine 200 ml water, 200 grams white sugar, and the peels of two lemons and bring the mixture to a boil. Stir until the sugar is dissolved then remove the syrup from heat. Let it infuse for 12 hours. Strain the syrup into a jar or other vessel.

CAPRI FIZZ

IRREGARDLESS
502 H STREET NE

Co-owner and sommelier Mika Carlin wanted this cocktail to capture the flavors of a caprese salad, a classic Italian plate with creamy mozzarella, fresh herbaceous basil, and bright tomatoes. It's the feeling of a warm summer afternoon in a glass.

GLASSWARE: Collins glass

GARNISH: Basil leaves

- 2 oz. Tomato Puree–Infused Gin (see recipe)
- ¾ oz. basil syrup
- ½ oz. heavy cream
- 1 oz. lemon juice
- 1 oz. egg white
- 2 dashes saline solution
- Splash of soda water

1. Add all of the ingredients, except for the soda water, to a shaker and dry-shake vigorously for about 10 seconds.

2. Add ice and shake for at least 15 seconds, until well chilled.

3. Strain the cocktail into a collins glass.

4. Pour a little bit of soda water back and forth between the empty halves of the shaker tins to pick up any residual cream and egg white, then use that to top the drink.

5. Garnish with fresh basil leaves.

MATCHA DO ABOUT NOTHING

IRREGARDLESS
502 H STREET NE

Espresso Martinis are everywhere these days, but the drink can leave you buzzing. For something a little easier on the nerves, the Matcha Do About Nothing at Irregardless swaps in matcha for a less-caffeinated take on the trend that will also appeal to the coffee-averse.

GLASSWARE: Coupe glass, chilled

GARNISH: Matcha powder

- 1 ½ oz. vodka
- ½ oz. elderflower liqueur
- 1 oz. concentrated matcha
- ½ oz. vanilla simple syrup
- ¾ oz. heavy cream

1. Add the vodka, elderflower liqueur, matcha concentrate, and vanilla simple syrup to a shaker filled with ice and shake until well chilled.

2. Strain the cocktail into a chilled coupe.

3. Garnish with matcha powder.

CHERRY WHISKEY SOUR

STICKY FINGERS DINER
406 H STREET NE

Sticky Fingers Diner owner and Food Network champion Doron Petersan says this fun pink vegan twist on a traditional Whiskey Sour is the most popular cocktail in the diner. Plus, she says, "Whiskey is for girls." Obtain the aquafaba by draining it from a can of chickpeas or other white beans.

GLASSWARE: Coupe glass
GARNISH: Luxardo cherries

- 2 oz. whiskey
- ¾ oz. Luxardo Maraschino Originale
- ¾ oz. fresh-squeezed lemon juice
- ½ oz. simple syrup
- 1 ½ oz. aquafaba

1. Add all of the ingredients to a cocktail shaker filled with ice.

2. Shake vigorously.

3. Strain the cocktail into a coupe glass.

4. Garnish with Luxardo cherries.

D.C. COCKTAILS — 201

NAVY YARD/
SW WATERFRONT

DC CRUSH

WET MONEY

HOTEL NACIONAL

Drinks with a water view are always in style. It's no surprise, then, that bars in these two riverfront districts draw steady crowds year-round. Both Navy Yard and the nearby Wharf development offer prime options for a day of cocktails by the river. Prices can be higher here (you pay for the atmosphere) and some national brands have planted flags, but there's quality to be found. There's no shortage of activities, either, as the Nationals and D.C. United home stadiums are in close range along with luxury shopping, dining, and hotels.

DC CRUSH

THE SALT LINE
79 POTOMAC AVENUE SE

Proximity to Nationals Park and a spacious riverside bar make The Salt Line a popular hangout during summer months. The menu blends favorites of the New England seacoast—think lobster rolls and fried clam bellies—with elements of the Mid-Atlantic region. In this cocktail, The Salt Line offers a frozen version of a Maryland beachside classic. A splash of locally produced DC Brau Orange Crush flavor notches up both the carbonation and citrus flavor. The recipe comes from Donato Alvarez, beverage director. Substitute any high-quality triple sec for the Luxardo Triplum.

GLASSWARE: Pint glass

GARNISH: Aperol float (optional)

- 1 (12 oz.) can DC Brau Full Transparency Orange Crush Seltzer
- 1 ¼ oz. Absolut Vodka
- 2 oz. orange juice
- 2 oz. white sugar
- ½ oz. Luxardo Triplum
- 1 oz. lime juice

1. Pour all of the ingredients into a blender. Keep the lid on but remove the centerpiece of the lid and cover the lid with a towel.

2. Blend briefly without ice to dissolve the sugar.

3. Add ice and blend until the ice has a smooth texture.

4. Serve with an optional float of Aperol on top for a slightly bitter version.

TODD THRASHER, TIKI TNT AND POTOMAC DISTILLING COMPANY

Todd Thrasher has been mixing up cocktails in D.C. for years, gaining notoriety for his work at PX Speakeasy in Alexandria in the mid-2000s and 2010s and, since 2018, for slinging tropical, beachy rum cocktails at Tiki TNT and distilling his own take on the spirit at Potomac Distilling Company.

How do you describe the cocktail culture of D.C.?

Being born and raised in the Washington, D.C. area, it's been amazing to watch the evolution of our cocktail culture, which continues to grow. From the time of speakeasies during the Prohibition era to opening a speakeasy of my own—PX—70 years later, bars have become essential gathering spots for urban neighborhoods scattered throughout D.C. The expansion to new areas of the city and beyond is exploding. Bars and restaurants are the cornerstones in these emerging localities.

Across our industry there is a strong sense of community that I really value. I host an annual cocktail competition at Tiki TNT, bringing together the top talents from behind the bar, all across the city. It's been a meaningful experience to help empower the next generation of mixologists. While I do not consider D.C. a "rum town," it is my plan to change that! Everyone loves a fun, beachy drink in the summer, but rum is progressing beyond this, becoming a mixing spirit in cocktails. My version of a Sazerac is made with rum and it's one of the more popular drinks that I serve.

What would you say is your signature as a bartender? What is the through line or philosophy that shapes your menus and concepts?

I think we all crave more interesting variations, but we don't want the process to be complicated. I love creating cocktails, but I no longer want the pomp and circumstance. At Tiki TNT, everything we do is with specific, precise formulas and recipes that keep our drinks balanced and flavorful. But our guests would not necessarily know the systems involved,

as the presentation is fun and carefree. Almost every cocktail we have has six different ingredients in it, but we've figured out how to quickly make a six-ingredient cocktail without sacrificing quality and taste.

What makes an outstanding bar program, in your opinion?

The goal is not to focus on what anyone else is doing. I think a lot of people will do things that they think critics may like or follow a trend. It should be the opposite. Know your customer. Listen and learn about what they look for in a drink and build on that to create a program that fits your style and your neighborhood. Establishing a loyal clientele speaks volumes and shows that you are delivering a trusted product.

If you met someone who was new to D.C., what advice would you give them for exploring the city's bars and neighborhoods?

I always suggest starting at The Wharf and not just because it is home to Tiki TNT. Situated just steps from the National Mall, it's the perfect entry point into exploring the city—food and drinks are a priority, and the best is here. With scenic waterfront views, it is home to 80 restaurants and shops, four hotels, and multiple venues to catch live music and performances. It's also pedestrian friendly so you can hop around from spot to spot, catching a drink and grabbing a bite while taking everything in.

WET MONEY

TIKI TNT
1130 MAINE AVENUE SW

Todd Thrasher is one of the handful of producers raising D.C.'s homegrown distilling profile. Tiki TNT is his homage to colorful, fruity, tropical, and often boozy beverages. Most spotlight a variety or two of Thrasher's Rum, his eponymous brand. Any of the drinks on the menu will put you in a good mood, especially given the bar's setting along the river.

GLASSWARE: Tiki mug or collins glass

- 1 ½ oz. passion fruit juice
- 1 oz. Espolòn Blanco Tequila
- 1 oz. Thrasher's White Rum
- ½ oz. lemon juice
- ¼ oz. blue curaçao
- 2 droppers salt water

1. Combine all of the ingredients in a cocktail tin with ice and shake well.

2. Strain the cocktail into a collins glass or tiki mug filled with fresh ice.

210 — D.C. COCKTAILS

HOTEL NACIONAL

COLADA SHOP
10 PEARL STREET SW

Imagine a deeper, fruitier daiquiri, round and ripe with notes of apricot and pineapple. That's the blueprint for the Hotel Nacional, a classic drink from Havana, Cuba. It's become a go-to order at Colada Shop, a Cuban cafe and cocktail bar with several locations in and around D.C. This rum-forward sour is especially appropriate for the cafe's small spot at the D.C. Wharf, a bustling and booming cluster of high-end local shopping and dining along the Southwest Waterfront.

GLASSWARE: Coupe

GARNISH: Dehydrated lime wheel

- ¾ oz. white rum
- ¾ oz. gold rum
- ¾ oz. pineapple juice
- ½ oz. lime juice
- ¼ oz. simple syrup
- ¼ oz. apricot liqueur
- ¼ oz. apricot puree

1. Add all of the ingredients to a cocktail shaker with ice.

2. Shake well, until chilled and combined.

3. Pour the cocktail into a coupe glass and garnish with a dehydrated lime wheel.

CHERRY BLOSSOM
SEASON

CHERRY BLOSSOM SPRITZ

CHERRY BLOSSOM OLD
FASHIONED

THE VIGNOLA SLING

Each spring, D.C. brims with anticipation for the arrival of its many cherry blossoms. The tradition started in 1912, when 3,020 cherry trees arrived in D.C. as a gift of goodwill from the Japanese government. All these years later, the peaceful trees and breathtaking blossoms have become ingrained into D.C.'s culture. The annual celebration inspires food and drink menus throughout the city as bartenders challenge themselves to find recipes that honor this special time of year.

CHERRY BLOSSOM SPRITZ

BLUE DUCK TAVERN
1201 24TH STREET NW

Located inside the posh Park Hyatt Hotel, Blue Duck Tavern is centrally located inside D.C.'s West End neighborhood, which, like much of the city, comes alive with colorful blooms early each spring. Evoking mild weather and fresh breezes, the bitter and aromatic notes of this low-ABV spritz celebrates Washington's popular annual Cherry Blossom Festival. It's simple to mix and ideal for a daytime drink, especially when enjoyed on the restaurant's patio.

GLASSWARE: Highball glass

GARNISH: Long orange peel, fresh cherry blossom flower

- 1 oz. Cappelletti Vino Aperitivo Americano Rosso
- 1 oz. Mancino Cherry Blossom Vermouth
- 4 dashes cherry bitters
- Club soda, to top
- Prosecco, to top

1. Combine all of the ingredients in a highball and add ice.

2. Top with equal parts club soda and prosecco. Do not mix or stir.

3. Garnish with a long orange peel and a fresh cherry blossom flower (if available).

CHERRY BLOSSOM OLD FASHIONED

BARREL
613 PENNSYLVANIA AVENUE SE

This dimly lit bar is a welcoming spot for anything whiskey, whether that's a shot and a beer, a pour of something fancy, or a well-made classic. As winter turns to spring, Barrel has been known to mix up this seasonal Old Fashioned, which uses Japanese whiskey in place of bourbon—a nod to the country of origin of D.C.'s famous cherry trees. For the whiskey base, Barrel uses Fuyu, a corn-based whiskey with qualities similar to bourbon.

—————————————— ✧ ——————————————

GLASSWARE: Rocks glass

GARNISH: Orange peel, brandied cherry

- ½ oz. Rose Water Syrup (see recipe)

- 2 oz. Japanese whiskey
- 3 dashes cherry bitters

1. In a cocktail shaker, combine all of the ingredients with ice and shake well.

2. Strain the cocktail into a rocks glass.

3. 3. Garnish with an orange peel and brandied cherry.

ROSE WATER SYRUP

Combine equal parts rose water and sugar in a saucepan. Heat the mixture to a gentle boil and stir constantly until the sugar is dissolved. Let the syrup cool before storing it in a glass jar.

THE VIGNOLA SLING

Inspired by Washington's famous cherry blossoms, this riff on a Singapore Sling blends tropical flavors with Italian spirits. For the name, Osteria Morini took inspiration from Vignola, a city in Italy's Emilia Romagna region that hosts the country's largest cherry blossom festival every spring. This springtime cocktail is both fruity and floral, tempered with Aperol's signature citrus-forward bitterness. The team of Sarah Vanags and Martin Mejia created this cocktail.

GLASSWARE: Hurricane glass

GARNISH: Orange peel and cherry on a skewer

- 1 ½ oz. Lockhouse Sakura Gin
- ¼ oz. Lazzaroni Maraschino Liqueur
- ½ oz. Aperol
- ¼ oz. Heering Cherry Liqueur
- ¼ oz. dry curaçao

1. Combine all of the ingredients in a cocktail shaker filled with ice.

2. Shake the mixture well until chilled and combined.

3. Double-strain the mixture over ice into a hurricane glass.

4. Garnish with an orange wheel hugging a cherry on a skewer.

MISCELLANEOUS/
FARTHER AFIELD

FINE CORINTHIAN COCONUT

PURPLETINI

SURFSIDE PIÑA COLADA

JALA-PIÑA BUSINESS

ANTIPASTI DIRTY MARTINI

MASSIMO'S ESPRESSO MARTINI

CHICCO'S CALABRIAN SPRITZ

MAURIZIO'S MIRTO COLLINS

JULIA CHILD'S MARTINI

Not all of D.C.'s cocktail bars fit neatly into a neighborhood. There are a number of notable bars stirring and shaking up drinks outside the city center or beyond metro-accessible locations. Here are several bars to consider making a stop at if you're in the area or want to explore Washington away from the beaten tourist path.

FINE CORINTHIAN COCONUT

TACO BAMBA
MULTIPLE LOCATIONS

As the name indicates, Taco Bamba is the place for tacos, and chef and owner Victor Albisu takes inspiration from every corner of the globe. That gives beverage director Amin Seddiq plenty to work with when building the bar menu. The Fine Corinthian Coconut borrows aspects of the Piña Colada and adds smoky mezcal with spicy and herbal notes from Green Chartreuse.

GLASSWARE: Beer glass

GARNISH: Toasted coconut, pineapple frond, flower

- 1 ½ oz. mezcal
- ¼ oz. Green Chartreuse
- 1 oz. pineapple juice
- ½ oz. fresh-squeezed lime juice
- 2 ½ oz. Coconut Milk Syrup (see recipe)

1. Place all of the ingredients into a shaking tin with ice.

2. Shake until chilled and combined.

3. Strain the cocktail into a beer can glass.

4. Garnish with toasted coconut, a pineapple frond, and a flower.

COCONUT MILK SYRUP

Combine 8 oz. granulated white sugar and 8 oz. coconut milk in a saucepan and cook on medium high until it starts to boil. Turn down the heat and let the mixture simmer for 5 minutes. Remove the pan from heat and let it cool. Label the syrup and store it in the refrigerator.

PURPLETINI

BAR IVY
3033 WILSON BOULEVARD, ARLINGTON, VA

Bar Ivy brings a West Coast–inspired restaurant and bar to the Northern Virginia cocktail scene. The Purpletini, a menu mainstay, is beverage director Ian Fletcher's play on the classic (but underappreciated) Aviation. Rather than use maraschino liqueur, Bar Ivy swaps in Lillet Rosé and gives the drink an overall slightly sweeter and more approachable profile.

GLASSWARE: Coupe glass

GARNISH: Lemon twist

- 1 oz. Empress 1908 Gin
- 1 ½ oz. Lillet Rosé
- ½ oz. crème de violette
- ¼ oz. Citric Water (see recipe)

1. Combine all of the ingredients in a cocktail shaker over ice.

2. Stir, then strain the cocktail into a coupe.

3. Garnish with a lemon twist.

CITRIC WATER

Stir together 15 grams citric acid with 8 oz. very hot (close to boiling) water. Let the mixture cool before using.

SURFSIDE PIÑA COLADA

SURFSIDE
4200 WISCONSIN AVENUE NW

No blender is required for this straightforward take on the Piña Colada. Instead, Surfside mixes up this beachy classic with a simple formula: aged Puerto Rican rum, high-quality coconut syrup, and pineapple juice. The 7-year rum does much of the work, carrying notes of oak and vanilla that bring depth of flavor, balance, and all the beachy feels. This recipe comes from Jared Smith.

GLASSWARE: Tiki mug or collins glass

GARNISH: Pineapple leaf

- **2 oz. Don Q Reserva 7 Rum**
- **1 ½ oz. pineapple juice**
- **1 ½ oz. Giffard Noix de Coco Syrup**

1. Combine all of the ingredients in a mixing glass with ice.

2. Shake, then strain the cocktail into a tiki mug or collins glass over fresh ice and garnish with a pineapple leaf.

CHACHO SPIRITS

Chacho Spirits took a non-traditional path to market, using a third-party distillery for production before opening its own distillery five years after launching. To hear co-founder Dan Ziegler tell it, the only way Chacho's brick-and-mortar facility became a reality was from all the support that bars and bartenders showed them during their beginning years. So, upon opening their own space, he knew he had to return the love. He did so by prominently featuring an "Around Town" section on the tasting room's cocktail menu, highlighting some of the D.C. bars that got them there.

The name "Chacho" was inspired by a trip to South America, where Ziegler fell in love with aguardiente, the national drink of Colombia. Named after a llama that he rode through the streets of Bogota after imbibing aguardiente for the first time, Chacho is a unique twist on the classic spirit, giving it a spicy jalapeño finish. The Chacho Spirits tasting room was a COVID-era labor of love, with the space built by hand by Ziegler and friends during quarantine before opening in May 2021.

JALA-PIÑA BUSINESS

CHACHO SPIRITS
6031 KANSAS AVENUE NW

Free State Bar, in D.C.'s Chinatown neighborhood, has been supporting Chacho Spirits since the early days, and bartender Jasmine Gailey has always been one of Chacho's biggest fans. "I was very excited when Dan [Ziegler] asked me to help create a cocktail for their menu," she says. The Jala-piña Business came about because I wanted something similar to a sour but that would allow Chacho's jalapeño flavor to really stand out, and the pineapple allows for the complexity of Chacho to really be the star."

GLASSWARE: Highball or coupe glass

GARNISH: Jalapeño slice and lime slice on a skewer

- 2 oz. Chacho Jalapeño Aguardiente
- 1 oz. pineapple juice
- ¾ oz. simple syrup
- ½ oz. lemon juice

1. Combine all of the ingredients in a cocktail shaker with ice.

2. Shake until combined and chilled, 30 to 45 seconds.

3. Strain the cocktail into a highball or coupe with fresh ice.

4. Garnish with a lime slice and jalapeño slice on a skewer.

ANTIPASTI DIRTY MARTINI

CARUSO'S GROCERY
914 14TH STREET SE

A t this red sauce joint, plates of Italian-American favorites like four-cheese garlic bread, chicken parmigiana, and penne alla vodka fly out of the kitchen. The bar program keeps pace with creative takes on classic cocktails. The Antipasti Dirty Martini has become a signature on the menu, a 1990's throwback of sorts that evokes the salty, savory, and slightly creamy flavor of a tomato, basil, and mozzarella salad. To get the mozzarella brine, take the liquid from a container of fresh mozzarella cheese.

GLASSWARE: Coupe glass

GARNISH: A skewer with one olive, one cherry tomato, and one small mozzarella ball

- 1 basil leaf
- 1 oz. Moletto Tomato Gin
- 1 oz. London dry gin
- ¾ oz. mozzarella brine

- ¼ oz. olive brine
- 2 dashes orange bitters
- Pinch salt

1. Put one basil leaf in the bottom of a cocktail shaker with ice, add the remaining ingredients, and stir for 25 seconds.

2. Strain the cocktail into a coupe.

3. Garnish with a skewer with one olive, one cherry tomato, and one small mozzarella ball.

MASSIMO'S ESPRESSO MARTINI

ITALIAN BAR
5008 CONNECTICUT AVENUE NW

Husband and wife duo Massimo and Carolyn Papetti are known for their dedication to Italian staples, both behind the bar and in the kitchen. Italian Bar brings the very European concept of the standing bar to D.C.'s Van Ness neighborhood. Aside from a couple of patio chairs, the action here happens at the long countertop bar. Customers can grab space to lean in and enjoy a quick snack or bite, like an espresso on the morning commute or a glass of wine or cold draft beer before or after dinner. This version of the Espresso Martini, created by bartender Maurizio Arberi, highlights the cafe's commitment to crafting the perfect shot of caffeine.

GLASSWARE: Coupe or martini glass

GARNISH: Shaved chocolate

- ¾ oz. Lucano Caffè Liqueur
- ¾ oz. Don Ciccio & Figli Nocino
- ¼ oz. hazelnut syrup
- ¼ oz. vodka
- 3 dashes chocolate bitters
- 1 strong shot of espresso

1. Build the drink in a cocktail shaker, with the espresso added last, then top with ice.

2. Shake vigorously until the shaker freezes.

3. Strain the cocktail into a coupe or martini glass. There should be two colors, with the darker espresso on the bottom and a rich, creamy head on top.

4. Garnish with shaved chocolate.

CHICCO'S CALABRIAN SPRITZ

I'M EDDIE CANO
5014 CONNECTICUT AVENUE NW

Quickly recite the name of this Italian restaurant and it'll sound awfully similar to "Americano." It's not just clever wordplay: it's an embodiment of how owners Massimo and Carolyn Papetti blend Italian and American cultures, both personally and in their businesses. Chicco's Calabrian Spritz is an homage to the nickname of the restaurant's corporate chef, Francesco. It gets Italian vibes from Italicus liqueur, limoncello, and prosecco, which I'm Eddie Cano serves on tap. This recipe comes from Maurizio Arberi.

✧

GLASSWARE: Wine glass

GARNISH: Lemon wheel

- ½ oz. Italicus Bergamotto
- ½ oz. limoncello
- ½ oz. fresh-squeezed lemon juice
- ¼ oz. gin
- 3 ½ oz. prosecco

1. Build the drink in a cocktail shaker with all of the ingredients, except for the prosecco. Top with ice and shake vigorously.

2. Strain the cocktail over fresh ice, preferably one large round rock, and top with the prosecco.

3. Garnish with a lemon wheel.

MAURIZIO'S MIRTO COLLINS

IN BOCCA AL LUPO
2400 WISCONSIN AVENUE NW

Expect Roman-style pizzas paired with original and classic Italian cocktails at this Glover Park neighborhood hangout. The bar and patio area both offer ample seating for sipping the thoughtful beverage list. In this highball, bartender Maurizio Arberi uses Wild Sardinia Mirto, made from myrtle berries. He also uses tequila, a rather uncommon spirit in Italian-focused bars.

GLASSWARE: Highball glass

GARNISH: 3 mint sprigs

- 1 ½ oz. tequila reposado infused with pepperoncino
- ¾ oz. Cocchi Sweet Vermouth
- ½ oz. Wild Sardinia Mirto
- ¼ oz. Faretti Biscotti Famosi liqueur

1. Add all of the ingredients to a mixing glass and top with ice.

2. Stir until the mixture is chilled and combined.

3. Strain the cocktail into a highball with fresh ice, preferably a single tall collins cube.

4. Garnish with three crisp mint sprigs.

JULIA CHILD'S MARTINI

SHOW OF HANDS
1401 PENNSYLVANIA AVENUE NE

Show of Hands is a craft cocktail bar nestled inside of The Roost, a multi-concept culinary clubhouse in Southeast D.C. that specializes in low-ABV cocktails and house-made spirits. This riff on a classic Martini was purportedly Julia Child's favorite Martini ratio, 5:1 vermouth to gin, the reverse of how it's normally prepared. High-quality dry vermouth from Cocchi really helps make it sing, and the German Gin from Ferdinand's is proofed down with Saar Riesling, adding a little florality that compliments the stellar vermouth.

GLASSWARE: Coupe glass, chilled

GARNISH: Lemon twist

- 2 ½ oz. Cocchi Vermouth di Torino Extra Dry
- ½ oz. Ferdinand's Saar Dry Gin
- 2 dashes orange bitters

1. Stir all of the ingredients together with ice until ice cold.

2. Strain the cocktail into a chilled coupe.

3. Garnish with a lemon twist.

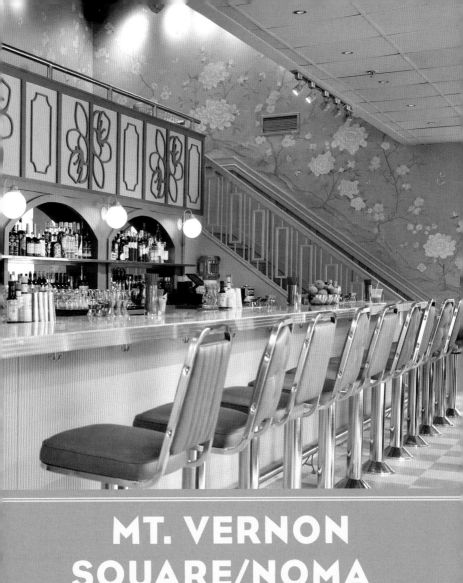

MT. VERNON SQUARE/NOMA

EASY PEASY!

NEW YORK SOUR

AFTERNOON SNOOZE

BANANA REPUBLIC

JAMAICAN HOLIDAY

FIG COBBLER

NEGRONI FUMO

9TH STREET CLOVER CLUB

Located to the North of Chinatown and south of Shaw, these adjacent neighborhoods are a hybrid of business travel, tourists, and locals. Mt. Vernon Square is where you'll find the city's convention center, a prime draw for out-of-towners. The urban environment can feel generic on the outside, but all the new construction has given way to a bar-going experience that's classic, refined, and a little over-the-top (in the best possible way).

EASY PEASY!

FOUNDING FARMERS & DISTILLERS
600 MASSACHUSETTS AVENUE NW

As the name suggests, this Gin Sour is a quick recipe to whip up when you're craving something crisp and refreshing. It uses the bar's own Founding Spirits Dry Gin along with subtle bitterness from Aperol and lemon juice. Muddled cucumbers add a summertime touch ideal for combating humid D.C. afternoons.

GLASSWARE: Nick & Nora glass
GARNISH: Cucumber wheel

- 2 cucumber slices
- 1 oz. Founding Spirits Dry Gin
- 1 oz. Aperol
- 1 oz. lemon juice
- ½ oz. simple syrup

1. In a cocktail mixing glass, muddle two cucumber slices. Add the remaining ingredients and fill halfway with ice.

2. Shake well until chilled and combined.

3. Strain the cocktail into a Nick & Nora, served up.

4. Garnish the glass with a cucumber wheel.

NEW YORK SOUR

FOUNDING FARMERS & DISTILLERS
600 MASSACHUSETTS AVENUE NW

Founding Spirits Bourbon is the canvas for this polished—not to mention photogenic—cocktail. The traditional Whiskey Sour gets an upgrade here with a red wine float that adds both a ruby-hued color and flavors of dark fruits and berries.

GLASSWARE: Old-fashioned glass

- 1 ½ oz. Founding Spirits Bourbon
- ¾ oz. simple syrup
- ¾ oz. lemon juice
- ½ oz. merlot

1. Combine all of the ingredients, except for the merlot, into a cocktail shaker tin. Add ice and shake.

2. Fine-strain the cocktail into an old-fashioned glass over fresh ice.

3. Float the merlot on top.

AFTERNOON SNOOZE

MORRIS AMERICAN BAR
1020 7TH STREET NW

Get the hammock ready and shake up this agave-spirit showcase that uses both clean, crisp blanco tequila and subtly smokey and earthy joven ("young") mezcal. Combine them with pineapple juice, lime, honey, and a couple drops of hot sauce, and you have the flavors of a lounging-by-a-tropical-beachside barbecue. This recipe comes from general manager Doug Fisher.

GLASSWARE: Coupe glass

GARNISH: Lime wedge

- 1 oz. blanco tequila
- 1 oz. mezcal joven
- ¾ oz. fresh pineapple juice
- ½ oz. lime juice
- ½ oz. honey
- 2 dashes Tabasco sauce

1. Combine all of the ingredients in a cocktail shaking tin with ice.

2. Shake until chilled and combined, about 15 seconds.

3. Strain the cocktail into a large coupe and garnish with a lime wedge.

BANANA REPUBLIC

MORRIS AMERICAN BAR
1020 7TH STREET NW

Banana-flavored drinks seem better suited for frozen cocktail machines than craft cocktail menus, but this take from Morris American Bar GM Doug Fisher ups the standard. Bottled-in-bond bourbon and dry vermouth provide a strong backbone to the sweetness of the banana liqueur and allspice dram.

GLASSWARE: Coupe glass

GARNISH: Lemon twist

- 2 oz. bottled-in-bond bourbon
- ½ oz. dry vermouth
- ¼ oz. banana liqueur
- ¼ oz. allspice dram
- 2 dashes Angostura bitters
- 1 dash orange bitters

1. Build the cocktail in a stirring glass, combining all of the ingredients together with ice.

2. Stir for 10 to 15 seconds and strain the cocktail into small coupe.

3. Garnish with a lemon twist.

JAMAICAN HOLIDAY

MORRIS AMERICAN BAR
1020 7ᵀᴴ STREET NW

I t's time to trade your flannel pajamas for a hammock and a mild breeze. This cheeky take on a holiday-spiced cocktail pairs traditional warming notes of maple syrup, apple cider, and grated cinnamon with beachy feels like a rich 8-year-old rum that's been amplified with a splash of overproof rum. Lemon juice and muddled mint complete the winter island fantasy.

GLASSWARE: Tiki mug

GARNISH: Mint flower, grated cinnamon

- 1 ½ oz. Appleton Estate 8 Year Old Reserve Jamaican Rum
- ½ oz. Smith & Cross Jamaica Rum
- ¾ oz. lemon juice
- ½ oz. maple syrup
- 1 oz. freshly pressed apple cider
- 8 mint leaves

1. Combine all of the ingredients, except for the mint leaves, in a cocktail shaker with ice.

2. Shake until chilled and combined, 10 to 15 seconds.

3. In a tiki mug, muddle the mint leaves and then fill the mug with crushed ice and the contents of the shaker.

4. Garnish with a mint flower and grated cinnamon.

FIG COBBLER

L'ARDENTE
200 MASSACHUSETTS AVENUE NW

Positioning itself as a "glam Italian" restaurant, L'Ardente doesn't hold back with flavor or presentation. Almost immediately after opening, it became known for its forty-layer lasagna, filled with paper-thin pasta and loaded with cheese and other ingredients. The bar program keeps up the energy from chef David Deshaies' kitchen, filling glasses with smoke, jellied booze, and other whimsical touches like the Caramelized Fig Syrup in this recipe.

GLASSWARE: Large brandy snifter, chilled
GARNISH: Mint bouquet, dehydrated lime wheel, powdered sugar

- ¾ oz. fino sherry
- ¾ oz. grappa
- ¾ oz. fresh lemon juice
- ½ oz. Caramelized Fig Syrup (see recipe)
- 3 oz. semisecco Lambrusco

1. Combine all of the ingredients, except for the Lambrusco, in a cocktail shaker.

2. Vigorously shake with ice for 10 to 15 seconds.

3. Strain into a chilled brandy snifter, fill with crushed ice, add Lambrusco to the glass, and gently stir to incorporate.

4. Garnish with a mint bouquet, dehydrated lime wheel, and powdered sugar.

CARAMELIZED FIG SYRUP

Pour 25 grams hot water over 50 grams demerara sugar and stir to dissolve the sugar. Add 25 grams fig puree and blend the mixture with an immersion blender until emulsified. Strain the syrup through a fine-mesh sieve and store it in the refrigerator for up to 2 weeks.

NEGRONI FUMO

L'ARDENTE
200 MASSACHUSETTS AVENUE NW

The cherrywood smoke wafting off L'Ardente's Negroni Fumo is accentuated by a base of mezcal, which takes the place of the standard dry gin. The drink also benefits from notes of rounded, nutty sweetness thanks to the addition of sherry. A gin-infused jello wedge adds a nostalgic (and boozy) garnish. You can substitute any red bitter liqueur for the Cappelletti.

GLASSWARE: Large brandy snifter, chilled
GARNISH: Expressed orange peel, cherrywood smoke, Negroni "Jello" Wedge (see recipe)

- 1 ½ oz. reposado mezcal
- ½ oz. Aperitivo Cappelletti
- ½ oz. sweet vermouth
- ¼ oz. Pedro Ximénez Sherry
- ¼ oz. Heering Cherry Liqueur

1. Combine all of the ingredients in a mixing glass with ice and stir for 30 to 40 seconds.

2. Strain the cocktail over a large ice cube into a chilled brandy snifter. Garnish with oil from an expressed orange peel.

3. Use a cocktail smoker to add cherrywood smoke to the snifter. Top the snifter with a small plate topped with the Negroni "Jello" Wedge and remove the plate when ready to enjoy.

4. Swirl the smoke and let it dissipate before sipping.

Negroni "Jello" Wedge

Halve and juice an orange, keeping the rinds to use as a mold. Blend the orange juice, 2 oz. London dry gin, 2 oz. hot water, 1 oz. Aperitivo Cappelletti, 1 oz. sweet vermouth, and 2 grams gelatin using an immersion blender until emulsified. Pour the mixture into one orange rind half and let the gelatin set in the refrigerator until firm. Slice the mixture (keeping it in the rind) into wedges and place one on a plate that fits snugly over your brandy snifter.

9TH STREET CLOVER CLUB

UNCONVENTIONAL DINER
1207 9TH STREET NW

The Clover Club, shaken with gin, raspberry syrup, and lemon, is underappreciated among classic cocktails. It's a great fit for Unconventional Diner, where chef David Deshaies's mission is to elevate simple, comforting dishes and drinks into something fun and unexpected. Here, the 9th Street Clover Club, named for the restaurant's address, is topped with a limoncello foam and fresh raspberries. You can substitute any white whine for the sauv blanc in the Limoncello Foam recipe.

GLASSWARE: Rocks glass, chilled
GARNISH: Limoncello Foam (see recipe), 1 fresh raspberry

- 1 ¼ oz. London dry gin
- ¼ oz. dry vermouth
- 1 oz. Sour Mix (see recipe)

- ½ oz. Raspberry Syrup (see recipe)

1. Pour the gin, vermouth, Sour Mix, and Raspberry Syrup into a cocktail shaker with ice.

2. Shake for 10 to 15 seconds, until all of the ingredients are incorporated.

3. Strain through a fine-mesh sieve into a chilled rocks glass filled with crushed ice.

4. Garnish the cocktail with Limoncello Foam and a fresh raspberry.

SOUR MIX

In a mixing glass, stir together 6 oz. lime juice, 6 oz. simple syrup, and 4 oz. lemon juice until combined. Store in the refrigerator until ready to use.

RASPBERRY SYRUP

Blend 4 oz. simple syrup and 8 oz. fresh raspberries using an immersion blender. Strain the syrup through a fine-mesh sieve and store it in the refrigerator for up to 1 week.

LIMONCELLO FOAM

Combine 6 oz. sauvignon blanc, 2 oz. simple syrup, 2 oz. limoncello, 1 oz. fresh lemon juice, and two egg whites and blend them with an immersion blender until fully incorporated. Pour the mixture into an iSi container (cream whipper). Charge the container three times with N_2O, shaking the container between charges, before using.

GEORGETOWN/
WEST END

DEATH IN THE AFTERNOON

"YO, YOU GOT BEEF?!"

CASTA'S MOJITO

GOLDEN GODDESS

POST WORTHY

SCANDALOUS

PUCKER UP

SMOKED WAGYU FAT-WASHED
OLD FASHIONED

KAMINEE DRINK

GETTING AL-SACY WITH
EVERYBODY

STUDY ABROAD SWIZZLE

FISH HOUSE PUNCH

Founded in 1751, Georgetown epitomizes classic Washington, D.C. Walking down the narrow streets, it's impossible not to imagine the power players that have lived in the neighborhood's iconic row homes and mansions. There is a sense of being disconnected from the central part of D.C. while also being incredibly tapped into the city's ethos of political and economic influence. That charm and romanticism brings plenty of crowds into Georgetown to shop and dine along its two main arteries of Wisconsin Avenue and M Street NW. Although some bars and restaurants here continue to stick to the textbook Washington feel, many new additions are pushing boundaries and becoming destinations for the entire city to enjoy.

DEATH IN THE AFTERNOON

APÉRO

2622 P STREET NW

The feeling of French sophistication is strong at this narrow Georgetown dining room and bar. Two of its signature luxuries, absinthe and Champagne, come together in bar manager Sean Meehan's take on a Death in the Afternoon, a cocktail with an origin story that traces back to author Ernest Hemingway's time in Spain. While the recipe typically uses only two ingredients—both alcohol—Meehan's version introduces a Lemon Oleo Saccharum that brings balance, brightness, and subtle sweetness to this bubbly concoction.

GLASSWARE: Nick & Nora glass

GARNISH: Lemon twist

- 1 oz. Mata Hari Bohemian Absinthe
- ½ oz. Lemon Oleo Saccharum (see recipe)

- 4 ½ oz. Champagne or Crémant, such as Côté Mas Crémant de Limoux

1. Combine the absinthe and Lemon Oleo Saccharum in a cocktail shaker with ice.

2. Shake, then strain the cocktail into a Nick & Nora glass.

3. Top with Champagne then garnish with a lemon twist.

LEMON OLEO SACCHARUM

Zest one lemon. Combine the lemon zest with 100 grams sugar and let the mixture sit for at least 2 hours. Add 100 grams hot water and stir until the sugar dissolves. Strain out the lemon zest and store the saccharum in the refrigerator until ready to use.

"YO, YOU GOT BEEF?!"

BOURBON STEAK
2800 PENNSYLVANIA AVENUE NW

The bar program at this upscale steakhouse is fitting of its location inside the Four Seasons hotel. Drinks don't come cheap, but they do come made with precision and creativity under the direction of Engidawork Alebachew. Among his favorite creations is the "Yo, You Got Beef?!," a play on a Manhattan that combines two of the restaurant's signature items: whiskey and steak. This recipe uses the restaurant's A5 wagyu fat as a flavoring base. Home bartenders also have the option to purchase wagyu tallow online or at high-end grocers. The drink is served tableside by smoking the glass with wood chips to bring out the nutty and rich flavors of the washed whiskey. The smoke also symbolizes how the kitchen cooks its steaks on a wood burning grill.

GLASSWARE: Coupe glass, chilled
GARNISH: Orange twist

- 2 oz. Wagyu Fat–Washed Bourbon (see recipe)
- 1 oz. sweet vermouth
- 2 dashes spice tincture

1. Combine all of the ingredients in a cocktail shaker filled with ice.

2. Stir for 30 to 45 seconds, until chilled and combined.

3. Strain the cocktail into a chilled coupe glass.

WAGYU FAT–WASHED BOURBON

Render 150 grams wagyu or beef fat/tallow over low heat and separate the solids from the liquids using a strainer or cheesecloth. Discard the solids. Mix the rendered fat with one 750 ml bottle of bourbon and let the mixture sit in the freezer for 2 hours. Once the fat freezes to the top, separate the solids from the liquid using cheesecloth and use the washed bourbon.

CASTA'S MOJITO

CASTA'S RUM BAR
1121 NEW HAMPSHIRE AVENUE NW

I f there's one drink a rum bar needs to make well, it's a crisp, clean Mojito. Casta's doesn't stray from the tried-and-true here, sticking to the base ingredients with white rum as the star.

GLASSWARE: Highball glass

- **Handful of mint leaves**
- **¾ oz. lime juice**
- **¾ oz. simple syrup**
- **2 oz. white rum**
- **Splash of soda water**
- **2 dashes Angostura bitters**

1. Muddle the mint, lime juice, and simple syrup in a highball glass.

2. Add the rum and ice and stir.

3. Top with a splash of soda water and the Angostura bitters.

GOLDEN GODDESS

CASTA'S RUM BAR
1121 NEW HAMPSHIRE AVENUE NW

The Golden Goddess blends spicy Margarita vibes with some tiki drink feelings from additions of falernum liqueur and homemade pineapple-jalapeno syrup.

GLASSWARE: Rocks glass

GARNISH: Dehydrated lime

- 1 ½ oz. Olmeca Altos Plata Tequila
- 1 oz. Pineapple-Jalapeño Syrup (see recipe)
- 1 oz. lime juice
- ¾ oz. falernum
- ½ oz. pineapple juice

1. Combine all of the ingredients in a cocktail shaker with ice.

2. Shake well until combined and chilled, about 10 to 15 seconds.

3. Strain the cocktail into a rocks glass over ice and garnish with a dehydrated lime.

PINEAPPLE-JALAPEÑO SYRUP

Combine 1 quart canned pineapple juice, 1 quart white sugar, and 1 sliced jalapeño pepper in a pot and bring the mixture to a boil. Lower the heat and let the liquid simmer for 15 minutes, then strain it into a heatproof container. Strain the syrup again and let it cool before use.

POST WORTHY

KINGBIRD

2650 VIRGINIA AVENUE NW

This Whiskey Sour, made with additions of ginger cordial and rose water, nods to the *Washington Post*, the newspaper that broke the story of the Watergate scandal in the early 1970s. This recipe comes from head bartender Kal Lemma.

$\diamond$

GLASSWARE: Collins glass

GARNISH: Fresh basil leaves

- 2 oz. Woodinville Whiskey
- ¾ oz. lemon juice
- ¾ oz. ginger cordial
- 2 drops rose water
- Handful of basil leaves

1. Add all of the ingredients to a cocktail shaker with ice.

2. Shake with ice until well chilled, 10 to 20 seconds.

3. Pour the cocktail into a collins glass and garnish with fresh basil leaves.

SCANDALOUS

The restaurant's namesake, the kingbird, is native to Washington, D.C. and can be seen perched along the Potomac River, looking for its next catch. This Martini turns heads when it comes out of the bar, thanks to Kingbird's bird-shaped glassware and the elaborate herb stem garnish that mimics tailfeathers. If you don't have a bird glass, a coupe will do. This recipe comes from head bartender Kal Lemma.

GLASSWARE: Bird glass

GARNISH: Thyme sprig, rosemary sprig, edible flowers

- 1 ¾ oz. blueberry and lemongrass–infused vodka
- ½ oz. apricot liqueur
- ¾ oz. Tarragon-and-Chai Cordial (see recipe)
- 1 oz. Champagne

1. Combine all of the ingredients, except for the Champagne, in a cocktail shaker with ice.

2. Shake until well chilled, 10 to 15 seconds.

3. Pour the cocktail into a bird glass or coupe, then add the Champagne.

4. Garnish with thyme, rosemary, and edible flowers.

TARRAGON-AND-CHAI CORDIAL
Add 300 grams tarragon powder, 150 grams masala chai tea mix, 1 liter of filtered water, and 1,000 grams of sugar into a pot and simmer at high heat until the sugar is dissolved. Lower the heat and stir for 5 minutes. Strain the cordial through cheesecloth or a coffee filter, then add 1 oz. vodka.

PUCKER UP

L'AVANT-GARDE
2915 M STREET NW

This cocktail is beverage director Hakim Hamid's riff on a traditional Negroni. Cognac replaces gin here, in line with L'Avant-Garde's French identity. In creating this drink, Hamid was inspired by Malcom X, Martin Luther King Jr., and Bumpy Johnson—three individuals with very different paths in life and different views but similar goals of peace and unity. This drink uses ingredients with different strengths that still come together in harmony.

GLASSWARE: Rocks glass
GARNISH: Expressed orange peel,
Pickled Sour Cherry (see recipe)

- 1 ½ oz. Monnet VSOP Cognac
- 1 oz. Cinnamon, Espresso Bean, and Vanilla–Infused Campari (see recipe)
- 1 oz. Carpano Antica Formula Vermouth
- ½ oz. Rothman & Winter Orchard cherry liqueur
- 2 dashes Fee Brothers Chocolate Bitters
- 2 dashes Fee Brothers Cherry Bitters

1. Combine all of the ingredients in a mixing glass, fill the glass with ice, and stir until well chilled and you achieve a dilution of about 25 to 30 percent.

2. Fine-strain the cocktail into a rocks glass over a large ice cube.

3. Garnish with an expressed orange peel and a carefully placed pickled sour cherry.

PICKLED SOUR CHERRY

Combine cherries, a lemon peel, a lime peel, a splash of red wine, a pinch of salt, a splash of Champagne vinegar, a splash of apple cider vinegar, and sugar, to taste, and allow the mixture to macerate for a minimum of 48 hours.

CINNAMON, ESPRESSO BEAN, AND VANILLA–INFUSED CAMPARI

To a liter of Campari, add 8 cinnamon sticks (about 1 oz. cinnamon), 2 whole vanilla beans, and a jigger of espresso beans and sous vide at 160ºF for 2 hours.

SMOKED WAGYU FAT-WASHED OLD FASHIONED

The D.C. location of this international Japanese and sushi restaurant puts a flare into its cocktails by using Japanese ingredients and flavors, like kuromitsu (black sugar syrup). This Old Fashioned gets a luxury turn in the form of wagyu fat-washed Japanese whiskey. This recipe comes from Filipe Bertrand.

GLASSWARE: Rocks glass, smoked with hickory (optional)

GARNISH: Kuromitsu, schichimi bacon

- 2 oz. Wagyu Fat–Washed Japanese Whiskey (see recipe)
- 2 barspoons kuromitsu
- 4 dashes umami bitters
- 2 dashes Angostura bitters

1. Combine all of the ingredients in a cocktail shaker filled with ice.
2. Stir for about 30 seconds.
3. Pour the cocktail into a rocks glass over a large ice cube.
4. Garnish with kuromitsu and shichimi bacon.

WAGYU FAT–WASHED JAPANESE WHISKEY

Render 150 grams wagyu or beef fat/tallow over low heat and separate the solids from the liquids using a strainer or cheesecloth. Discard the solids. Mix the rendered fat with one 750 ml bottle of Japanese whiskey and let the mixture sit in the freezer for 2 hours. Once the fat freezes to the top, separate the solids from the liquid using cheesecloth and use the washed whiskey.

KAMINEE DRINK

Rasika's West End outpost is the place to be in D.C. for modern, artful Indian cooking in a sleek and modern setting. Its Kaminee Drink spices up the classic pairing of Pimm's No. 1 Cup liqueur and London dry gin by using a chile pepper infusion and adding bright pops of lemon and ginger.

GLASSWARE: Highball glass

GARNISH: Cucumber round

- **1 oz. Pimm's No. 1 Cup**
- **1 oz. Chile-Infused Gin (see recipe)**
- **1 oz. ginger syrup**
- **1 oz. fresh lime juice**

1. Combine the Pimm's, gin, ginger syrup, and lime juice in a cocktail shaker filled with ice and shake.

2. Strain the cocktail into a highball glass filled with ice.

3. Slide a radius into the cucumber round so you can twist it into an S-shape as a garnish.

CHILE-INFUSED GIN

Split three Thai green chile peppers and let them infuse in a 750 ml bottle of London dry gin for 3 days.

GETTING AL-SACY WITH EVERYBODY

THE SOVEREIGN
1206 WISCONSIN AVENUE NW

Ordering a cocktail at The Sovereign might seem like a secondary choice in the face of the extensive Belgian beer list stocked with rare finds. But know that the bar also leans into Belgian booze and ingredients. This refreshing cocktail—a base of gin and genever along with elderflower and ginger liqueurs—is The Sovereign's best seller.

GLASSWARE: Rocks glass

GARNISH: Lemon wheel

- ¾ oz. London dry gin
- ¾ oz. jonge genever
- ¾ oz. elderflower liqueur
- ½ oz. dry vermouth
- ½ oz. ginger liqueur
- ¾ oz. lemon juice

1. Combine all of the ingredients in a cocktail shaker with ice.

2. Shake hard and strain the cocktail into a rocks glass.

3. Add rocks and garnish with a lemon wheel.

STUDY ABROAD SWIZZLE

THE SETTING
2512 PENNSYLVANIA AVENUE NW

I f you weren't looking for The Setting, you'd likely miss its unassuming entryway next to Market Street Diamonds. The bar's name is a nod to the jewelry store above, and the drinks, service, and food here have a feel that's both luxe and relaxed.

Bar manager Michael Fratt cut his teeth as part of some of D.C.'s best cocktail teams. That includes stints at Service Bar and Barmini, among others. This creation of his traces the history of the French Carthusian Monks who were expelled from the cathedral where they created Green Chartreuse, one of the spirit world's premier botanical liqueurs. These monks fled to Spain between the late 1700s and early 1900s, where they discovered Spanish ingredients like saffron and tarragon—ingredients that led these same monks to invent the softer, more mellow Yellow Chartreuse. The recipe here substitutes the rum base of a traditional Swizzle with that legendary Yellow Chartreuse and nutty Amontillado sherry. Along with the rest of the components, like falernum, pineapple, and honey, it adds up to an eminently crushable cocktail.

◇

GLASSWARE: Hurricane glass
GARNISH: Mint sprigs, straw

- 1 oz. Yellow Chartreuse
- 1 oz. Amontillado sherry
- 1 oz. lime juice
- ¾ oz. pineapple juice
- ½ oz. falernum
- ½ oz. honey syrup
- 6 to 8 mint leaves

1. Swizzle all of the ingredients together in a hurricane glass with crushed ice.

2. Top the glass with crushed ice.

3. Garnish with fresh mint sprigs and a straw.

FISH HOUSE PUNCH

THE FOUNTAIN INN
1659 WISCONSIN AVENUE NW

The Fountain Inn is a reimagining of an eighteenth-century Georgetown tavern. Originally founded in 1783 by John Suter, the bar's new life began in 2021. The cozy space is filled with rare and vintage spirits fit for splurging, including plenty of old whiskeys and other curiosities. Behind the bar, general manager Morgan Kirchner and her team revive some of the less-appreciated cocktails from America's history, along with seasonal recipes.

This drink was named after the Philadelphia fishing club, the State in Schuylkill, where it was first concocted in 1732. George Washington was famously unable to write in his diary for three days after overindulging in Fish House Punch at a victory celebration. The Fountain Inn house twist is a lower-ABV version that replaces some of the booze with bright citrus so you can still enjoy your weekend. Note that golden syrup is caramelized simple syrup.

GLASSWARE: Rocks glass
GARNISH: Grated nutmeg

- 1 oz. blanc vermouth
- ¾ oz. decaf Earl Grey tea
- ½ oz. Swedish Punsch
- ½ oz. lemon juice

- ¼ oz. cognac
- ¼ oz. peach liqueur
- ¼ oz. Barbados rum
- ¼ oz. golden syrup

1. Combine all of the ingredients in a cocktail shaker with ice.

2. Shake until combined and chilled.

3. Strain the cocktail into a rocks glass over ice.

4. Garnish with freshly grated nutmeg.

PENN QUARTER/ CHINATOWN

SALT AIR MARGARITA

MEDIA COMINACION

PROJECT MANHATTAN

THE OLD POND (FURU IKE YA)

SESAME MARTINI

Although you'll see Chinatown noted on city maps, its influence here is smaller than in other major cities. The main indicator is the Friendship Archway at the intersection of H Street NW and 7th Street NW. Businesses in the neighborhood also include Chinese lettering on their signage. To the south and west is Penn Quarter, a dense patch of prime eating and drinking. It's here that you'll find the nucleus of chef, restaurateur, and humanitarian José Andrés' restaurant group, along with plenty of other exciting internationally inspired mixology.

SALT AIR MARGARITA

OYAMEL
401 7TH STREET NW

Few drinks in D.C. are as iconic as this Salt Air Margarita. The foam-like topping has been delighting guests for years and is an essential order when at Oyamel, chef José Andrés's outpost for modern (and fun) Mexican cooking. The glassware suggestion here is for a Martini glass, but you can change that if you prefer.

GLASSWARE: Martini glass

- 1 ½ oz. tequila
- ¾ oz. Combier Liqueur D'Orange
- 1 oz. lime juice
- ¾ oz. simple syrup
- Salt Air (see recipe)

1. Place all of the ingredients, except for the Salt Air, in a shaker tin and fill the larger tin halfway with ice.

2. Shake until frost forms on the outside of the tin.

3. Use a strainer to pour the cocktail over a martini glass.

4. Use an immersion blender to activate the Salt Air.

5. Using a large spoon, scoop a top layer of the Salt Air and float it over the cocktail.

SALT AIR

Combine 22 oz. water, 11 oz. lime juice, 5 tablespoons salt, and ½ table-spoon sucrose in a container large enough to stir them with a whisk until the sucrose and salt are dissolved. (For best results, add the salt and sucrose to warm water until dissolved, adding the lime juice when the water is at room temperature.) Keep the Salt Air in a container that allows for an immersion blender to agitate the mixture later.

MEDIA COMINACION

According to Jaleo, this drink has a story as one of the—if not the—most classic aperitif cocktails from Madrid, although not very well known by the younger generations. The name, translating to "half (size) combination," is thought to have originated from the recipe's blending of the Jai Alai (gin, vermouth, and soda) with the El Colonial (vermouth, Picon, curaçao, Angostura bitters, and mint). In Spain, the drink is usually ordered in its half-size version due to its strength, especially considering that this is often consumed as a little break in the day in which people still have to function and work. A caña is a half-size collins glass.

GLASSWARE: 7 oz. caña glass

GARNISH: Expressed orange peel, lemon wheel

- 1 ¾ oz. Yzaguirre Rojo Reserva Sweet Vermouth
- ¾ oz. Fords Gin
- ½ teaspoon Cynar
- 2 dashes Angostura bitters

1. Combine all of the ingredients together in a cocktail shaker with ice.

2. Throw the ingredients, tossing them back and forth several times between the cocktail shaker and tin. (Stirring is also an option.)

3. Strain the cocktail into a caña glass over one large ice cube.

RYAN CHETIYAWARDANA, "MR. LYAN," SILVER LYAN

Silver Lyan cocktails are on the one hand extremely precise and creative and on the other, just really good and fun drinks. How do you find that balance?

One of the things that I've really loved about all of our bars is that all of our team is super experienced. It's not like you're in a weird restaurant where the team can only make what's part of their mise-en-place in front of them. The beauty of a bar is you can serve anything. We've got curated back bars of spirits, but all the teams are so adept at knowing that, sometimes, all you really need is a great Gin and Tonic, or a Negroni, or a Manhattan.

We get to have our menus that tee up some of the more fanciful stuff and give people the opportunity to step outside their comfort zone a bit. But we can also always knock up something a little more classic. Coming to the U.S. was really exciting around that, because people here are much better grounded in cocktails. The average person makes a great Martini at home.

How do you describe your through-line of bartending and hospitality?

Each of our venues has a different character and really plays to its location. For us, it's always been about how we can use storytelling to help the hospitality of the bar. "Theme" sounds too heavy, but the focus of each of the bars, it's all a little different.

We love what we do, but the last thing we want is to be preachy about it. The reason we use some of the language on the menu about the drink style or what situation it suits is that we want to be able to get a drink to you as soon as possible. And we're pretty speedy in the way that we work. If you want to know stuff, we're there to tell you. Everything's got a story, but ultimately we're not there to ram it down your throat.

What's been your experience in D.C., and how do you describe the city's bar culture?

With all of our expansion, we only did things that felt authentic to us and that would fit the city. It had to be for the city; that was the primary point about it. It wasn't just about doing a cookie cutter transporting of something we've done before. It was about creating something that was specific.

We did so much research for the opening here. I flew back and forth—it was a joy. The reason that we opened here was because I fell in love with the city. I saw what was going on and thought it would be wonderful to be part of that—and not to just go and opportunistically plug something in. It's been amazing and it's really lovely to see how we've been received by not only the food-and-drink crowd, but the public, as well.

D.C. is unexpected in all sectors. But it's also the prettiest city I've been to in the U.S. You get that idea of the closeness of it and the balance of lots of different sides. It's a city that punches above its weight but also feels super close to things, and that to me is reflected in the food and drink. It's homely and close and you feel like you're part of somebody's vision, but it's on a level that is international. I often talk about how I compare this city to Edinburgh. I lived in Edinburgh for a long time and it was a food and drink scene that I think people overlooked for a long time and then when you go there, everything is amazing.

What tips would you give to home bartenders?

One of the things I always say to my friends is that you need way more ice than you think you need. It's a key ingredient that I think people overlook. The other is that a lot of people default to trying to project a menu or a set of drinks—that might be a theme to a party or it might be something that's really en vogue at the moment. My main suggestion is to use what you love. If you've got a load of tequila in your liquor cabinet it's probably because you love tequila. Use what you primarily have. And then from there, keep it simple.

PROJECT MANHATTAN

SILVER LYAN
900 F STREET NW

The Project Manhattan has been a staple of Silver Lyan since the bar's opening in 2020. The drink is both simple and a bit unusual, especially for a luxury hotel bar. Originally inspired by Mr. Lyan's Nuked Negroni, the process of microwaving the drink deeply integrates all the flavors of the cocktail very quickly, resulting in a richer, more harmonious take on the classic Manhattan. Silver Lyan bartenders emphasize that using the specific spirits called for is very important to the final flavors of the cocktail.

GLASSWARE: Coupe glass, chilled
GARNISH: Maraschino cherry

- 1 ½ cups Westward Single Malt Whiskey
- 1 ½ cups Laird's Bonded Apple Brandy
- 1 ½ cups sweet vermouth
- 4 ½ tablespoons blackcurrant liqueur
- 15 drops Angostura bitters
- 1 cup water

1. Combine all of the ingredients in a closable, microwave-safe container.

2. Microwave the mixture on medium power three times in increments of 1 minute.

3. Transfer the mixture to a bottle and store it in the freezer.

4. To serve, pour 3 oz. into a chilled coupe and garnish the cocktail with a maraschino cherry.

THE OLD POND (FURU IKE YA)

CRANES
724 9TH STREET NW

This cocktail is one of Cranes's top sellers, as it embodies the restaurant's blend of Spanish and Japanese flavors and cultures. The inspiration behind the cocktail was chef Pepe's ajo blanco, which was a twist on a traditional Spanish cold soup with almonds, apples, and green grapes. Sommelier Ferit Ozergul set out to create a light and smooth cocktail with similar flavors, supported by the Japanese spirit shochu. Iichiko Saiten is made from barley and, at 43% ABV, is a bit stronger than most. The Old Pond is also clarified with milk to give it a silky mouthfeel and more complexity. This process also makes the cocktail shelf stable. This recipe makes a batch of 10 cocktails but can be made in smaller or bigger batches.

GLASSWARE: Rocks glass
GARNISH: Dehydrated apple slice with paprika

- **12 oz. milk**
- **15 oz. iichigo Saiten Shochu**
- **15 oz. freshly squeezed Granny Smith apple juice**
- **7 ½ oz. orgeat**
- **5 oz. freshly squeezed lemon juice**
- **3 oz. yuzu juice**

1. Pour the milk into a 60 oz. or bigger container.

2. Mix all the other ingredients in a separate container, then pour the mixture over the milk.

3. Close the lid and refrigerate the container overnight, ideally 24 to 48 hours.

4. Filter the mixture slowly through a coffee filter. Wet the coffee filter ahead of time and don't try to press to get better results. Filtering can take some time, but it's worth the wait.

SESAME MARTINI

Tonari features a unique culture combination, bringing together Japanese and Italian cuisines and techniques. It sounds odd at first, but there are many similarities. Both countries know a thing or two about noodles, for one. Known for their "wafu"-style cooking, Tonari is a carb-lovers paradise for its pastas and pizzas that borrow ingredients from East and West. The bar is no different, and beverage director Laggy Batjargal's Sesame Martini is an ideal representation of what Tonari does so well. The herbaceous drink has a warm nuttiness and was inspired by the Embrasse de la Terre cocktail created by Zachary Faden, winner of the 2017 Tales of the Cocktail Official Competition.

GLASSWARE: **Martini glass, chilled**
GARNISH: **3 to 4 drops sesame oil**

- **1 oz. Beniotome Sesame Shochu**
- **1 oz. Malfy Gin Originale**
- **¾ oz. Dolin Dry Vermouth**
- **¼ oz. Yellow Chartreuse**

1. In a mixing glass filled with ice, combine all of the ingredients and stir for 30 seconds, until combined and well chilled.

2. Strain the cocktail into a chilled martini glass and garnish with the sesame oil.

PHOTO CREDITS

Pages 14–15 by Saltbridge Strategies for Barrel; page 23 by Jennifer Chase; page 27 courtesy of The Imperial; pages 28, 31, 43, 175, 185, 186 by Rey Lopez; page 33 courtesy of The Green Zone; page 35 courtesy of Le Mont Royale; page 37 by Mack Ordaya; pages 46–47 by Melena DeFlorimonte; page 49 by James C Jackson; pages 51, 155, 160, 237, 245, 288 by John Rorapaugh for LeadingDC; page 53 courtesy of Eric Hilton & Cory Llewellyn; page 55 by Mykl Wu; page 57 courtesy of Jane Jane; pages 59, 61 by Fernanda Aburdene; pages 67, 69 by David Strauss; page 70 by Tracy Eustaquio; pages 72, 75 courtesy of Rooster and Owl; pages 77, 79 courtesy of Purple Patch; pages 85, 87 by Hawkeye Johnson Photography; page 89 by Stacey Windsor/Boundary Stone; page 91 courtesy of The Dabney; page 95 courtesy of The Royal; page 103 courtesy of Service Bar; page 105 by Fredde Lieberman; page 106 courtesy of Lucy Bar DC; pages 113, 114, 116 courtesy of Buechert's Saloon; pages 119, 207 by An Phuong-Ly; pages 121, 123 courtesy of The Wells; page 129 by Aphra Adkins; page 131 by Jill Collins PR; pages 133 and 135 by Versus; page 136 by Jennifer Chase; pages 139, 142–143, 271, 279, 281, 293 by Travis Mitchell; page 144 by courtesy of Round Robin Bar; page 150 courtesy of The Jefferson Hotel; page 153 by Michael Collins Photography; page 157 courtesy Ellington Park Bistro; page 159 by Saltbridge Strategies for McClellan's Retreat; page 163 courtesy of Lyle's; page 169 by Naku Mayo; pages 171, 173 courtesy of St. Anselm; page 176 courtesy of Cotton & Reed; pages 178, 180 courtesy of Destino; page 183 by LeadingDC; page 193 courtesy of Stable; pages 197, 199 courtesy of Irregardless; page 200 by Deb Lindsey; page 209 by Jon Thorpe; page 211 courtesy of Tiki TNT; page 213 courtesy of Colada Shop; page 219 courtesy of Blue Duck Tavern; page 222 courtesy of Osteria Morini; page 229 courtesy of Taco Bamba; page 231 courtesy of Bar Ivy; page 232 courtesy of Surfside; page 234 by Plush Marketing Agency; page 239 courtesy of The Italian Bar; page 240 courtesy of I'm Eddie Cano; page 242 courtesy of In Bocca Al Lupo; pages 246–247 courtesy of Morris American Bar; pages 251, 253 by Ken Fletcher; pages 254, 257, 258 by Jamie Mackey; pages 261, 263 by Mike Fuentes Photography; page 265 courtesy Unconventional Diner; page 273 courtesy Bourbon Steak; pages 275, 277 courtesy Casta's Rum Bar; page 283 courtesy of L'Avant-Garde; page 285 courtesy of Nobu DC; page 287 courtesy of Rasika West End; page 299 by Reema Desai; page 300 courtesy of Jaleo/José Andrés Group; page 305 courtesy of Silver Lyan; page 307 courtesy of Cranes; page 308 by Vina Sananikone.

Pages 1, 3, 4–5, 8, 18–19, 38–39, 62–63, 80–81, 92, 96–97, 101, 108–109, 124–125, 146–147, 164–165, 188–189, 195, 202–203, 214–215, 220–221, 224–225, 266–267, 290–291, 294–295 used under official license from Shutterstock.com.

Pages 4, 9, 10–11, 12, 13, courtesy of Library of Congress.

ACKNOWLEDGMENTS

This project has been the culmination of more than a decade of work writing about and celebrating the D.C. cocktail community. I am so grateful to the team at Harper Collins and Cider Mill Press for entrusting me with this project and recognizing all that D.C. bars and bartenders have to offer. I am incredibly thankful for my editor, Jeremy Hauck, who kept everything (especially me) on track throughout the process and shaped this book into the best version of itself. I would like to recognize all of the editors and publishers that have supported me and my work over the years, helping me to sharpen my voice and allowing me to get to where I am today. Thank you again to my wife, Jamie Mackey, for her tireless encouragement and for being the best plus one around. And finally, know that this book would not have been possible without the superb talent and dedication of the D.C. bartending family. I raise a glass to you all. Cheers.

ABOUT THE AUTHOR

Travis Mitchell moved to Washington, D.C. in 2007, earning a Bachelor's Degree in journalism from American University. He has spent the years since exploring and writing about the city's vibrant bars, restaurants, and neighborhoods. His work has appeared in digital and print outlets including *Eater DC*, *Thrillist DC*, *District Fray* magazine, *The Washington Post*, *The Washington City Paper*, and more.

INDEX

—About Cider Mill Press Book Publishers—

Good ideas ripen with time. From seed to harvest, Cider Mill Press brings fine reading, information, and entertainment together between the covers of its creatively crafted books. Our Cider Mill bears fruit twice a year, publishing a new crop of titles each spring and fall.

"Where Good Books Are Ready for Press"
501 Nelson Place
Nashville, Tennessee 37214
cidermillpress.com